Schooling for Tomorrow's America

A volume in
Research in Curriculum and Instruction
O. L. Davis, *Series Editor*

Schooling for Tomorrow's America

edited by

Marcella L. Kysilka
University of Central Florida

O. L. Davis, Jr.
University of Texas–Austin

INFORMATION AGE PUBLISHING, INC.
Charlotte, NC • www.infoagepub.com

Library of Congress Cataloging-in-Publication Data

Schooling for tomorrow's America / edited by Marcella L. Kysilka, University
of Central Florida, and O.L. Davis, Jr., the University of Texas at Austin.
      pages cm. – (Research in curriculum and instruction)
   ISBN 978-1-62396-355-2 (pbk.) – ISBN 978-1-62396-356-9 (hardcover) –
ISBN 978-1-62396-357-6 (ebook) 1. Public schools–United States. 2.
Educational change–United States. 3. Educational planning–United States.
4. Education–Aims and objectives–United States. I. Kysilka, Marcella L.,
editor of compilation. II. Davis, O. L. (Ozro Luke), 1928- editor of
compilation.
   LA217.2.S377 2013
   370.973–dc23

                                                    2013019219

Copyright © 2014 Information Age Publishing Inc.

Printed in the United States of America

CONTENTS

ACKNOWLEDGEMENTS

This book would not have been possible if it were not for the efforts of the History Committee of the Centennial Celebration of Kappa Delta Pi. The committee deemed it important to publish a book authored by a group of our Laureates who were willing to look toward the future of education in the United States. In addition to the efforts of the History Committee members and the authors of the chapters in this book, we would also like to thank Kappa Delta Pi for supporting the project as an important contribution to educational thinking in the twenty-first century.

—OLD, Jr
—MLK

FOREWORD

I like to read everything about education. Articles about education tend to make me think, question, wonder, ponder, and occasionally laugh out loud. Whether the article reaffirms my own beliefs, or causes me cognitive dissonance, if it is about education, I want to read it. I ask myself, and then my students, questions about what is read. "Who is this author?" "Is this research or opinion, and how do we know?" "How did this person become an authority in the field, and, with fame, does his/her writing change the work in schools?" "If we had this author in our room today, what would we ask him/her?" "What might we implement in our own classrooms from this reading?" "What research might we want to do, based on what we have read?" I hope you ask these questions as you read this book.

This book can be read by educators at all stages in their careers. What a great selection for a book study group of practicing teachers or for a seminar with graduate students. The authors share their thoughts about education for the future, but also inform us about the past. Whether you encounter this book as a textbook or for a professional learning community, the contents will inform and inspire you, encouraging you to think deeply and work towards the improvement of education.

I first read the work of some of the authors of this book when I was a doctoral student. These authors were just names to me then, names to be dropped in that final oral exam if I wanted my degree. Then, something amazing happened. I joined an organization where the people whose work I had read actually appeared and spoke. I heard speeches from the authors about their backgrounds, experiences, and work. Then, even more

Schooling for Tomorrow's America, pages ix–x
Copyright © 2014 by Information Age Publishing
All rights of reproduction in any form reserved.

amazing, I met and had conversations with these people. I served on a board with a few of them. Wow! As a colleague quipped, "it's like we are meeting our rock stars." Kappa Delta Pi is that organization.

As you read these chapters, think about the content of the pieces, and about the careers of the authors. Reflect upon your education, your career in teaching, and where you are going next. Consider how Kappa Delta Pi, an International Honor Society in Education, can help connect you (virtually and maybe even in person) to educational leaders who are making a difference. Start to write about your teaching and your experiences. Maybe our next book will have your chapter in it. It's all possible.

—**Mary C. Clement**, 2012–2014 President, Kappa Delta Pi
Professor, Teacher Education, Berry College, GA

PROLOGUE

In 1990, Kappa Delta Pi published the book, *Honor in Teaching: Reflections.* I was the editor of that publication and I suggested, during my presidency 1986–1988, that we ask our Laureate members to contribute to a book that would pay tribute to the thousands of teachers who daily influenced students to do their best, to work hard, to participate fully in their education. These were tough times for the teachers and the students. I described the situation: "People in the field of education were angered, perplexed, astonished, and exasperated by the constant criticism from various governmental agencies, the public, and yes, their own colleagues, about our public education" (p. vii). What was going on? The 1980s were a time of national reforms. The reform reports were brutal; our elementary schools were failures because the children could not read; our secondary schools were failures because the students did not "measure up favorably to their foreign counterparts"; and "our universities were graduating mediocre products, students who could not function adequately in their chosen professions" (p. viii). The criticisms were published not only in our professional literature, but in the public press. There were programs on national television that focused on our terrible schools and the calls for reform came from parents, the media, the schools, the government, and anyone who thought they had something pertinent to say, much of it printed in the public press and numerous "popular" literature. Teachers worked hard to teach the students amid the horrendous criticisms of their inadequacies. The environment was pretty toxic. Yet, there were great teachers in great schools doing great things. Students were succeeding, even in those schools that

Schooling for Tomorrow's America, pages xi–xiii
Copyright © 2014 by Information Age Publishing

were struggling because of changing demographics, lack of adequate funding, and dysfunctional families. I concluded that "because our schools are painted as bastions for failure, the public had little regard for the quality of our schools or for the people who devote their lives to the education of the children" (p. viii–ix) . . . the teachers.

Thus, I proposed that we ask the Laureates to address three fundamental questions: How can we convince the public that our schools are not fortresses of failure? How can we gain the respect we so rightfully deserve as teachers? How can we restore honor to the teaching profession? Fourteen of our Laureates responded to my challenge: Robert Anderson, Ernest Boyer, Harry S. Broudy, William Carr, Elliot Eisner, Ned A. Flanders, Arthur W. Foshay, John Hope Franklin, William Friday, Theodore M. Hesburgh, Alice Miel, Harold G. Shane, Ralph W. Tyler, and William Van Til. Their essays were refreshing and inspiring . . . they provided us with hope.

Now it is 22 years later, and in many ways, not much has changed with respect to the public's perceptions of our public schools. We are *still* being harshly criticized for the inadequacies of our education. More and more demands are being placed upon our schools to "fix" what society and parents have not been able to do . . . that is, we need to not only "educate" the students, but we must provide for their moral, social, personal, and interpersonal, nutritional, psychological, sexual, and intellectual development. That is a full plate by anyone's standards and we are expected to do that with less support and more stringent criteria for success—most of it in the form of high stakes testing that really does not measure all that teachers are expected to accomplish with their students. Yet, the teachers diligently attend to their charge—they go to class everyday, they plan their lessons, they motivate the students, they counsel the students, they interact with the parents, they constantly learn new strategies, they participate in professional meetings and in-service training, and they struggle with the daily challenges of teaching because they care: They want the students to have every opportunity for success; they want the students to have a wonderful life, to follow their dreams, to become model citizens; and they want the students to achieve the American Dream!

As a member of the History Committee of the Centennial Convocation Planning Committee of Kappa Delta Pi, I supported the idea of once again asking our Laureates to provide words of wisdom to us, but this time, not to look back on what we have accomplished, but to look forward to what lies ahead—to provide us with words of encouragement, to open new vistas, to celebrate the achievements we have made and can still make, to explore the wonders of possibilities for change and growth. We are in need of a good "shot in the arm" to renew our enthusiasm for the future of education and all that it can provide for American youth.

Dr. O. L. Davis, Jr., a Laureate and member of the History Committee, volunteered to contact the current Laureates and requested an essay from them that looked to the future. As a result, we have gathered eleven essays that provide us with intriguing and challenging thoughts about the future of education. I hope you read them, think about them, share them, and perhaps take the time to reflect on your own thoughts about the future of education and the roll you can play in that future. Educators are an essential and integral part of the future of education in this country. They need to find their voices, to speak up, to inform the politicians and the public about the importance of education to the future of America.

—Marcella L. Kysilka
Co-editor

CHAPTER 1

PUBLIC SCHOOLING IN HARD TIMES

Adaptation and Invention Remain Possibilities

O. L. Davis, Jr.
The University of Texas at Austin

These are the times that try men's souls
—Thomas Paine, *Common Sense*, 1776

It was the best of times. It was the worst of times
—Charles Dickens, *A Tale of Two Cities*, 1859

Americans currently endure a ruptured economy, polarized politics, and a possible future of continuing warfare abroad. The American sense of community that we once shared appears now to be fractured; seemingly beyond repair. Others of us, mainly people of color, never held full membership in that community and most continue to live near but not sufficiently inside its invisible but quite real boundaries. Our public schooling mirrors the general society and, thus, shares most of these troubles and others that relate to them.

Schooling for Tomorrow's America, pages 1–20
Copyright © 2014 by Information Age Publishing
All rights of reproduction in any form reserved.

We Americans also hold memories, however fragile, of hard times that previously engulfed our society and its schools during as well as across specific periods of our national history. We remember, as well, episodes, and ideas and legislation that different ones of us believe helped our society and schools not only to survive but also to overcome, at least in part, especially exasperatingly hard times that we have known.

This essay identifies some of the forces that powerfully constrain the efforts of contemporary American public schooling to contribute more fully to the education for America's future. Also analyzed are aspects of these enfeebling circumstances. Importantly, it offers hope for a revival of the vigor of public schooling within the gloom of present realities. Admittedly, the essay draws heavily upon my reflective lived experiences, scholarly research, and thoughts during my long career of intimate involvement in American public education.

A POLITICAL ECONOMY OF DESPAIR AND THE CORRUPTIONS OF BELIEFS

The provision of schooling in America, unlike in most other nations, has been a matter of state responsibility and control since the establishment of the nation's constitution. This commitment to local control of schooling has fostered the development of local school districts that are charged to conduct schooling under usually general guidelines and structures. Until recently, the federal government has not been involved in the organization, conduct, oversight, and funding of local schools. Nevertheless, substantial rhetorical support of American public schooling ordinarily has emphasized its contributions to the nation and the continuance and improvement of the general American experience. School funding, additionally, has been justified primarily on its asserted contributions to general citizenship. Its major constraint has been the very uneven distribution of taxable sources between the several states and between school districts within states. Public schooling in the American states admittedly has never been funded well enough and, most commonly, only at barely proximate adequacy.

Harold Benjamin, a Kappa Delta Pi Laureate and distinguished educator, chose to comment about American parsimonious school funding with a homespun anecdote. Americans, he insisted, liked to praise the value of the nation's schools to its economic prosperity and political prospects, but, as if they were shooting dice in a game of craps, they would seek to run the house on a two-bit (25 cents) bet.

These present times, however, bear witness to a profound change in state funding of public services. The rhetoric of politicians and business and industrial leaders continues to tout the virtues of schooling, indeed the critical need for significantly improved education especially because of the high expectations of intense international economic competition. However, state gubernatorial and legislative decisions, backed by these same business leaders, have reduced the percentage of state funding for the operations of public education. Likely, never before in the history of the republic has American public schooling suffered so grievously from such reductions. The political outlook for a reversal of this recent pattern, moreover, appears extremely dismal at best.

Admittedly, the total number of dollars appropriated for public schooling in several states during recent legislative sessions typically has risen slightly, but these increased sums appear to be due to continued inflationary pressures and ordinarily have represented stunning decreases in the percentage of state support directed to that schooling.

Such decreased funding is not limited to public education. Funding for other state and local services also has suffered decreased support. Responsibility for these decisions reasonably may be laid at the feet of a recently developed political orthodoxy that advocates severely restricted governmental actions and the concurrent reduction or elimination of taxes to support those few actions and some very few other services.

State and local governments and school districts must offer some public services mandated by federally enacted programs (e.g., medical care for uninsured persons, aid for children of impoverished parents, care for mentally handicapped individuals). These programs appear to require increasingly large shares of available state revenues. In the absence of raising taxes, the only real option for governors and legislators is to reduce the percentage of available monies allocated to different state programs.

The most commonplace results of these actions on state services, including public schooling, have been crippling and have devastated many local districts' budgets for routine operations. At the same time, school districts across the nation have found themselves unable to increase local taxes because of local political pressures as well as state regulations. In such situations, the prospects for the careful maintenance, not to mention possibilities for improvement of public schooling, can only be reckoned as politically unlikely or very grim. American public schooling is in the midst of very difficult financial times.

To be sure, the federal government has made available some funds to states during the past half-century to be used by schools for targeted and limited purposes, For example, as a response to Cold War priorities, the National Defense Education Act (1958), provided funds to improve science and mathematics programs; its renewals, and similar measures. Federal funds always have been supplementary, never foundational, and, in large measure, piecemeal, almost never continuing.

Likewise but in particular, the notorious No Child Left Behind (NCLB) Act brought some new amounts of federal funds to states and local schools for quite limited purposes. It also brought something else: increased and active federal intrusion into the expectations and operations of public schooling in local school districts and states of the nation. This new and profoundly changed federal activism, in company with its attendant requirements, constituted a momentous sea change in federal-state relationships. Federal funds arrived with special, freshly minted mandates, among them requirements for national curriculum standards and publicized league tables of students' achievement test scores that have been passed off with mischievous results to the general public as school results (or, in economic terms, products or outputs). To be sure, a few states already had developed their own new (and, as self-touted, tougher) standards with accompanying state-wide testing and mandated ranking of individual schools by pupil achievement accompanied by widespread publication of these results. Even these states, however, in order to receive the new federal funds, had to junk or seriously modify their self-initiated efforts to comply with federal mandates for the new and claimed more rigorous "national" standards for schooling with sets of punishments for schools whose students scored lower than federal legislators' and bureaucrats' expectations for their achievement.

Additionally, most state legislatures have required in recent years the expansion of a number of programs (e.g., bilingual education, pre-school programs, and reduced pupil-teacher ratios). Too many of these initiatives failed to provide increased funding to pay for their additional expenses. Thus, these "unfunded mandates" at the state level exacerbated administrative problems and created new pressures on local school budgeting which included consideration of or actions to eliminate teacher positions as well as general teacher benefits such as health insurance premiums, as well as to axe school programs (e.g., music, art, library, and physical education) that suddenly had become "non-essential" because of sharply diminished local budgets.

In such unfavorable circumstances, can a bright future for public schooling be imagined? Does a very restricted and harsh economy dictate that school offerings become fewer, poorer, and less related to the lives of students and the America in which they will live in the future? In the face of substantial despair, I will argue that schooling for tomorrow's America can be brighter than many of the current conditions appear to predict. Most importantly, adaptation and innovation are possible. Nevertheless, we need to consider several other conditions that cloud contemporary schooling.

THE DECLINE OF POPULAR SUPPORT
OF PUBLIC SCHOOLING

The persistent erosion of support for the American public education enterprise constitutes a particularly vexing situation. Especially attacked has been the once widely held belief that public schools were appropriate for the preparation of all young Americans... all the children of all the people... to engage fully in their society, to enter advanced studies as they were qualified and interested, as well as to learn that useful information that would enable them to engage in productive work as adults.

This understanding, long articulated but flagrantly unfulfilled across some 200 years for Black children and children of some but not all immigrants/groups, receives current emphasis in snappy slogans, but with substantially reduced passion and programs. Contemporary Americans routinely find much about which to complain about the operations of public schools in general, but polls across a number of years reveal that citizens commonly express satisfaction and pride in the schools of their own communities. They typically applaud the efforts and interests of local teachers and administrators to offer high quality instruction even as they believe that American schooling has declined for at least the past half-century and that students in schools of other nations exceed American students in achievement in basic school subjects.

As early as the 1920s, a swelling tide of public criticism focused on the asserted dreadful shortcomings of progressive education, its core ideas and techniques. What began as reasonable concern and calls for substantial schooling at all levels of the enterprise escalated into routinely misrepresented charges about contemporary schooling, especially since World War II. Although still noticed, a number of these claims diminished as their spokespersons sought explanatory power in quite a number of typically unsubstantiated charges.

For example, much early twentieth century school architecture (particularly that of high schools) represented to the community a kind of local "cultural temple" for most citizens. The school building was a center for the perpetuation of democracy, whether in small rural towns or in major cities. Following World War II and the school construction crisis of the period, school boards increased local taxes to pay for construction of additional structures to accommodate increasingly larger enrollments of school age children and youth. During those years, many opponents of the increased taxation necessary to fund new construction harshly criticized local school leaders as free-spending officials intent on building "palaces" rather than less expensive, but serviceable structures. One result of this opposition was the creation of school landscapes that featured undistinguished "big boxes" that resembled factories and retail and storage facilities more than they emblemized centers of civic pride and of learning in a democratic society.

These post-war years also featured highly publicized incidents in which a few strident and belligerent critics levied scorn on public schooling because of their misshapen perception that public school teachers were indoctrinating school children in communistic and atheist positions, about concerns that teachers lacked substantive background and "training" in the subject matters that they taught, and that American schooling was "out of date," failing, and seriously lagged behind schooling in other countries, therefore perilously jeopardizing the future of our nation. Most of these disputes, disturbing as they were in local settings, were settled in short order by reasonable negotiation and innovation. In some other locales, one or more concerns escalated into forms of cultural warfare that persisted for years, some of which attracted national notice, but these clashes ordinarily subsided after a time with few "winners," but with serious casualties to reputations and roles, ravaged human relationships, and censored or abandoned curricula (e.g., core programs, Man: A Course of Study [MACOS curriculum]), and textbooks. The major issues in these charges simply became dormant and remembered by only a few members of the community.

Support for public schooling in America has eroded, also, as political efforts to secure public funding for private schooling has increased. For more than a century, this issue featured attempts by supporters of parochial, mainly Roman Catholic, schooling to secure public monies for their operations. This concern seldom involved the funding of non-sectarian, private schools. In no small measure, the issue divided Americans along religious lines. With Catholic children, particularly in large cities, attending parochial schools, public schooling in many of those communities became a near-protestant schooling. The general problem increasingly became complicated as efforts swelled to separate specific religious observances and direct instruction about religious knowledge from public school teaching and observances.

Across years, advocates of increased and improved public schooling have understood the bleak reality that available funds to support public schooling were very limited and that competition for legislative funding (by states and by the federal government) of private and/or parochial schools predictably would result in even less money available for public schooling. This basic problem took on special complexities in the wake of the *Brown versus Board* decision that public schools could not segregate school attendance by race. Quickly following this court ruling, numerous southern Whites responded to the decision by withdrawing their children from public schools and enrolling them in hastily organized, private, mostly protestant or independent Christian church-affiliated academies that enrolled only White children and youth.

Particularly, this development has also become the case in several parts of the nation in which new, private sector, faith-based schools have become popular. These developments have proceeded hand-in-hand with the related advocacy of charter schools, essentially private schools (i.e., ones exempted from many state regulations), but funded operationally by state grants. "Systems" of charter schools sited across a region or state are a recent development. The companion offering of state-wide schooling carried by television and the internet (i.e., virtual schools) signals the dawn of competing state systems of public education. Much of these new political emphases have been generated by a general anti-government, no/low taxing sentiment that holds that private operations simply are superior and foster better results than do public schools, derisively dubbed "state schools."

SCHOOLING AS HUMAN CAPITAL DEVELOPMENT

Coincident with these types of opposition to public schooling, the understanding of schooling as "human capital development," advocated by notable conservative economists, has become influential. Many prominent business and political leaders accept this notion as a changed purpose of public education. The theory is simple and attractive. Schools exist primarily to develop the human capital (children and youth) needed by the nation in order for it to continue its leadership (or domination) of world affairs. In this view, schooling that stresses general education does not prepare students for jobs that currently exist nor jobs that business and industry likely will develop in the future. This circumstance, so goes the argument, constitutes an unwise decision for both students and the nation. In order not "to waste" human capital, education in specialty subjects, primarily in mathematics and science, should begin early and continue throughout pupils' schooling. Subjects in other curriculum areas in this schema might be offered to especially talented children and youth, but for most other students, such courses would not "pay off" either to the larger society or to the individuals.

This notion of school purpose is not at all identical to and only very slightly related to the calls for vocational education for increased numbers of students. That nineteenth and early twentieth century concern targeted not all students, but mainly only some students; for example, individuals who because of financial constraints could not continue schooling past high school and who needed marketable skills in order to enter the nation's paid workforce, students whose ambitions, aptitudes, and achievement seemed not to predict their reasonable success in post-secondary schooling, and students of lower class backgrounds.

Within the rhetoric of "human capital development," the central concern has shifted profoundly from the needs of students to the needs of the society at large. Public schooling, in this new advocacy, appears appropriate only or primarily for the preparation of young people who can profit from early and continued programs that "feed" the anticipated needs of business and manufacturing upon which the long term future of the nation assuredly depends.

This new conceptualization appears to be advocated essentially as an antidote to the ills that pester today's American business enterprises. Never before have American business leaders insisted that the nation require a special program of public schooling to ward off international competition. Maybe, businesses really do not need such a program at all. Perhaps, their current advocacy of this idea has more to do with a desire to decrease expenditures for public schooling (and the costs in taxes paid by businesses to support that schooling) than it has to do with the prospects of the future successes of American businesses. This speculation may be cynical, but it can be dismissed only at the risk of substantial peril.

Such an advocacy, moreover, disgraces the history of the American people and their institutions as well as it substitutes a near fascist "what is good for society is good for individuals," for the democratic ethos of "what is good for individuals likely will be good for the society." This newly articulated position offers a servant economy to the nation whereas an industrial economy fostered "manual training" and "vocational education" in the late nineteenth and early twentieth centuries and a "service economy" called for "career education" in the mid-twentieth century. None of these emphases caught the attention of a majority of Americans of those times. The importance of individuals within community in American schooling and their individual decision making about their life's work fits neatly into the conventional American dream. The idea of someone in authority making an individual's decisions regarding their life work is alien to that dream.

The misshapen notion of "human capital development," nevertheless, has attracted widespread support to become a second prominent purpose, even if a contradictory purpose, of public schooling. It neatly fits the folk-wisdom contained in commonplace language. For example, as the aphorism goes, if teachers (schools) teach, then students learn. If student do not learn, then teachers (schools) did not teach them and schools fail at very high economic costs to society. This over simplistic, brutal, and illogical notion remains profoundly wrong-headed. Nevertheless, the appeal appears to have struck an appreciative chord with a citizenry that seeks sure results of schooling of all students without regard to their capacities and interests and without allocation of increased public funding for education. In a very short period of time, legislative and management mandates in many states have replaced former guides for improvement; penalties of different sorts and magnitudes became legislative remedies for the claimed failures of teachers and schools as well as for students whose scores on state mandated texts were lower than those that state governors, legislators, and education bureaucrats had insisted that they be. Centralized bureaucratic control swiftly became the means of state and federal enforcement of compliance with the mandates, even though most of the mandates illogically chose the wrong targets.

Sparked by these recent mandates, students rhetorically became "products" without regard to their personal attributes related to school achievement as well as without consideration of the extent of their engagement with teaching and their assignments. Students, therefore, who failed to learn what schooling offered them, have been re-conceptualized as individuals who are not at all responsible for their own achievement. Students, in this conceptualization, came to be understood as victims of rather than as necessary, active participants in their own failed schooling. In this flawed mindset, students came to school eager to learn the school offerings and to achieve as high as was possible, but schooling (and teachers, specifically) failed to teach them. Our society could rescue students, schooling, and the American way of life, according to the advocates of this new point of view by the employment of two easily established procedures; ones assumed to be prevalent and determinative in private industry. And huge sums of money also could be saved in the process.

One means to determine if schooling in a state, or, even in the nation, was creating "achieving learners," would insist on the simple analysis of students' scores on achievement tests tied to grade level and course objectives. Such a move would verify or dispute the claimed purpose. Moreover, inasmuch as students' abilities and backgrounds wrongly can be assumed to be common across ages and grade levels, their scores on the state achievement tests would be recognized, albeit illogically, as "school scores."

Schools judged to be "failing" would be penalized by public censure and, if these results persisted, their teachers and principals could be dismissed and replaced by "good teachers" and "good principals." Furthermore, schools themselves could be closed if their "failing" position persisted across a defined period of years. The recent history of such applied policies reveals many misadventures and seemingly intractable problems that easily should have been foreseen.

Clearly, this movement was and remains irresponsible. Its advocates almost never admit the huge financial costs of the development of state-wide grade-level and course objectives, construction and validation of individual test items and of the yearly tests, the scoring of tests and the reporting of test scores and analyses. These expenses may be "just normal" as is often asserted, but they typically remain crudely estimated or unspecified. At present, in Texas, these real costs are expected to rise to almost one billion dollars a year in current prices within just five years. Furthermore, the costs to individual teachers and pupils in time lost from teaching and studying to the preparation of pupils for the testing sessions, as well as the increased external pressures on them have had the effect of de-skilling both groups, appears not to have been either anticipated or calculated. The costs, according to general teacher estimates, are huge. The proposals of this movement appear to have been advanced without any serious consideration of the very real and substantially high costs of the tests themselves, the creation of unanticipated and expensive system disturbances, and the likely ruinous impact on teachers' self-worth and dedicated service. And these costs do not include damages to individual students' efforts, sense of accomplishment, and personal identity.

Much more devastating even than these matters is the general failure of Americans to recognize that students' "outcomes based" learning profoundly confuses teacher and/or school intention with cause. This particular failure is part of a general failure of logic and the companion willingness to apply unsound logic to some other but not all "influential" settings. This corrupt idea is analyzed further in the subsequent section, "For Educators, A Special Mission: To Think Clearly and to Speak Directly and Responsibly" (pp. 15–19).

Seen in these lights, the crux of the hard times currently endured by American schooling can be known primarily as "political." To be sure, other factors including, for example, historical, economic, and cultural matters have been and are present in Americans' imaginations of and in their policy decisions about the future of schooling in this nation. For much too long a period of time, Americans—and especially American educators—appear to have wanted to keep the educational enterprise separated from and "uncontaminated" by politics. This self-induced dream world simply did not and does not relate at all to the reality of American life.

Men and women, for example, who serve on local boards of education with credentials that support or oppose various dimensions of schooling and whose intentions are soundly grounded toward meaningful public service are, first of all, human beings. They bring with them to board meetings their sympathies toward and reservations about all manner of personal and community concerns. In their deliberations, these concerns influence the contexts and formats and substance of their decisions, from designation of school attendance zones, interests in the school use of the newest electronic communication devices, concerns about the continuation, upkeep, and/or renewal of the district's planetarium, swimming pools, playgrounds, and athletic playing fields, to issues about desired teacher-pupil ratios to be sought for the coming year's operations. Politics in public schooling has been and is present. Such politics must be present. This politics will continue to be present. We educators share the obligation to make politics work for the education of children and youth and the development of our society.

And, surely, costs routinely must be recognized by us educational professionals as practical, even necessary, considerations about schools' curricular and instructional plans and practices for every year. Certain and possible costs cannot be avoided in decisions about schooling. Trade-offs between patently desirable options likely cannot be avoided without off-setting decisions about other matters considered somewhat less worthy or, perhaps more commonly, ones that also are deemed as worthy as those under consideration for elimination. These types of policy considerations are not just the politics of hard times; they are commonplace and reasonable elements of the educational politics of all times.

American public schooling is enmeshed in exceedingly hard times... again. Teacher morale and effective school functioning across the nation continues to disintegrate, although at various rates, in response to individual and group perceptions of recriminatory policy rhetoric, legally compulsory and, often, administrative mandates, and reduced resources.

Career teachers have heard most of the negative (and derogatory) comments for years. These barbs continue to sting and belittle teachers' contributions. "Teachers have it easy; three months off every year... and with pay, too," some citizens cavalierly claim. And, to be sure, "Why can't bad or inadequate teachers be fired?" Also, "We know that teachers should have a salary increase, but our district budget is cut to the quick... and we already have had to release teachers. Our citizens will not approve a tax increase for any purpose. Teachers, in the main, typically "soldier on"; they continue to do the best that they can with the resources that they have.

Generally known is that educator compensation is the largest single component of local school budgets. Therefore, to reduce school budgets almost assuredly requires either salary cuts for teaching personnel or the reduction in numbers of teachers. To slash school budgets almost certainly will require both actions. And, such actions carry predictable costs. Class sizes may be expected to balloon to numbers unknown since the aftermath of World War II when 60 children were commonplace in many elementary school classrooms and 45 or more adolescents routinely packed high school classes. Some consequences of such policy actions easily are predictable. In my home community, failure to pass a four cent tax increase this fall will trigger a decision to close two elementary schools, the possible elimination of 20 teachers from district's rolls, and raise class sizes in all the remaining elementary schools. Similar circumstances appear on the horizon for many districts across the nation. In all likelihood, numerous veteran teachers simply will leave the profession. Some who are eligible will retire. Others will seek alternative employment. These teachers will decide that the current political and educational milieu in which they find themselves is too onerous in which to continue to teach.

Additionally, the teaching profession will become increasingly less attractive to high ability individuals who might consider teaching as a career. Like all pupils are not equally endowed with the same motivation, intelligence, background opportunities, and creativity, so, also, are all teachers different in those personal characteristics that relate importantly to teaching success. Students, under the best of circumstances, should not be treated to identical instruction. Neither, in a near-perfect world, should all teachers receive salaries and benefits identical to other teachers with similar preparation and teaching experience. Our world is not perfect, however, and group trade-offs for reasonable but less than appropriate individual compensation has made sense in order to prevent capricious administrative actions to punish or reward teachers on grounds other than competence. Furthermore, a host of scales and efforts to measure teaching competence as a means of administering differentiated salary payments have been tried in practice and usually have failed resoundingly. To wage efforts to justify and effect salary differentiation appears fruitless and counterproductive in these particular times of severely reduced school budgets and legislated enactments of increased demands on teaching practice.

In such times, is public schooling destined only to wither and perhaps disappear from the American scene? Currently, a prominent politics of despair emphasizes the pressing need to reduce government expenditures in general, with national defense the only possible exception and even its mindless support has shown prominent fissures. Public schooling has escaped, so far, being explicitly targeted for elimination. On the other hand, the politics of despair refuses to entertain tax increases, the only means by which government can have funds for public expenses. This situation raises the specter of an American landscape absent several vital public services. One of those services could become, in some short time, public schooling. This calamitous prospect appears to be the product of an excited imagination as well as a loss of confidence in the American dream. Surely, this vision, sometimes called the American spirit, is robust enough to outlast, even overcome this current pessimism. Still, we must acknowledge that we who support public schooling appear to see through a glass, darkly. Our anxiety certainly narrows our perceptions of reality and clouds our ability to imagine possibilities. Importantly, we must take seriously the charge to invent, within community, a future for public schooling that is robust, inviting of high expectations for individual students, consistent with the natures of school subjects as well as the nature of our abiding culture, and offered, as George Peabody called his philanthropic benevolences to education in the American South following the Civil War, "a debt due from the present to future generations" (1869).

PERCEIVING OPPORTUNITIES
WITHIN THE PERSISTENCE OF HARD TIMES

Ralph Tyler, one of our profession's greatest scholars and spokespersons during the twentieth century, keenly understood the nature of hard times in education.

In his role as a Kappa Delta Pi Laureate during the decades of the 1970s and 1980s, he spoke often at Society gatherings. Most of his remembered addresses emphasized a key point. Some of education's greatest innovations came as intellectually challenging and quite inexpensive responses to the hard times that enveloped public schooling of the depression period. Serving as his most prominent examples were the in-school and in-classroom developmental work and research conducted as part of what became known as the Eight-Year Study during the 1930s. Almost all of us listeners expressed surprise at Professor Tyler's optimism. Here was an imminent scholar who was telling us not to do what others had done during other periods of hard times. Instead, he shared his confidence that, individually and collaboratively, we in our own times could invent means by which to better teach by focusing on something that we could do.

Each of us who has studied accounts of the Eight Year Study has favorite elements of its initiatives. Among my favorites are core programs in secondary schools; students' on-site investigations of conditions of poverty, unemployment, and relief; rigorous student investigations of propaganda by government and businesses; students' use of photographs, newspaper articles, and radio programs to communicate findings of their serious and sustained inquiries to interested, mature audiences, ones who might use the information to effect some local change; and, even, the transition of a school yearbook from an unwieldy large compendium to a narrative-based, book-length account of real students and teachers who had worked on important group and personal learning projects and activities during an entire school year and which were published by a trade book issued by a major national publisher. Most of Tyler's listeners, even ones who knew nothing of the Eight-Year Study, imagined ideas for teaching that they believed they could undertake or for which they could begin to plan within days or a few weeks.

Professor Tyler was right. Knowledge of successful endeavors in any times commonly motivates others to perceive elements in situations that they have not before seen. And hard times need not prevent teachers, students, and administrators from inventing educational futures in their schools that others had never before perceived as possible. Perceived "obstacles" are roadblocks. On the other hand, beginning to think of possibilities appears to be a kind of master key to the invention and launch of new and productive ventures.

"PUSHING BACK" AGAINST THE CLAMOR
FOR RIGIDITY AND SAMENESS

For more than a dozen years, waves of mandates have insisted that every American student must post arbitrary minimum scores on asserted tests of competence in school subjects at every grade level. Public "push back" against this unwelcomed reign of external imposition and *statism* (i.e., federal and state centralization and control) is increasing. Among other concerns, classroom teachers were among the first to criticize these requirements. They rapidly recognized that large segments of teaching time were being diminished, even sabotaged, by the increased time allotted for testing. Especially during the past year, many school superintendents and other officials have joined with parents and some few politicians and business people to mount pushbacks against over-testing in schools. The extent of this pushback seems to be small at this time. Nevertheless, that this opposition has arisen at all is significant. That it has taken more than a decade to take form and voice is sobering.

Not to be lost in this welcomed development is that these pushback efforts seem not to be simplistic. And, they should not be. Moreover, they insist on serious, active participation of educators in school reforms rather than their scholarship, experience, and commitment to more robust, stronger schooling being ignored by the public peddlers of school reform ideas. Teachers share the recognition that pupils' test results are important, but they quite properly recognize and advocate that such results should be used to inform educator decisions about next steps in instruction rather than primarily as a bludgeon with which to harass and punish teachers and students for their judged shortcomings. Although this pushback action only recently has begun, it appears to be hobbled by its timid expression of unwillingness to involve larger numbers of the entire community, not simply a few arbitrarily identified "stake-holders," in deliberations intended to strengthen public schooling.

Additionally, these pushback actions appear to be characterized by weak analyses and over-cautious rhetoric to describe the reality of the oversight and management of the imposed mandates. More effective pushbacks surely will be characterized by bolder interpretations of data. We can be certain that those who favor public schooling as human capital development will use a great variety of means by which to obstruct or to dissipate the force of recent pushbacks against curriculum uniformity and rigidity of instruction.

Needed pushbacks can only be sustained, if at all, by increased knowledge of educational programs and effects. For example, increased instruction of students ordinarily yields increased, not diminished, variance in pupils' test scores. Differently stated, increased high quality instruction should anticipate increased differences between students' school achievement, *not* increased sameness between the school achievements of different students. Simply, recent attempts to seek standardization and sameness of student achievement results are wrong and counterproductive. They also constitute types of "road maps" that lead only to educational catastrophe.

FOR EDUCATORS, A SPECIAL MISSION: TO THINK CLEARLY AND TO SPEAK DIRECTLY AND RESPONSIBLY

Educators must face up to a specific responsibility. We simply must think clearly about the realities and prospects of public schooling in all times. We cannot stand as spectators on the sidelines of public debate about education. This responsibility is one theoretically shared with many others who would influence public schooling. We must grasp this responsibility even if some in our communities step aside or if others do not attend it seriously and deliberatively. We cannot wish away this responsibility even though most of us educators are grievously unprepared for this kind of public participation. Our preparation programs, for example, stressed our talk with students, almost never talk with adults (e.g., parents, administrators, and other citizens). Most of us will have to learn as we go along. Thinking clearly and expressing ourselves powerfully in public discourse have not been routine expectations of professional practice. Now, however, we must think clearly and express ourselves powerfully as elements of our daily practice.

Educators really have no viable option in this matter. We know intimately the vagaries and regularities of educational practice. We are part of the "everydayness" of the details of public schooling. We have rejoiced as our students have grasped an idea or skill and embraced it as their own. And we have witnessed the deaths of possibilities as students decide that they have no reason to try to engage a set of fresh constructs unrelated to anything in their personal experience. We have recognized the erosion of students' motivation by the unavailability or scarcity of demanding materials and assignments. We must become partners in innovations and reforms. Routinely uninvited to the public square at which issues are probed and possibilities are examined, we nevertheless must gain entrance to the deliberations. We must contribute our experience and knowledge.

Our insistence to be participants likely will be opposed. Our society's history is that teachers do not and should not act in policy decision-making. Rather, teachers are and should be only acted upon. This severely corrupt notion must not persist as Americans struggle their way out of the current hard times. No one can empower another; such a notion is foolish as well as illogical. Individuals never are *given* power. Individuals take power; they *assume* it. Note, for example, the perplexity and distress of parents when their children act differently from the ways that parents have "prepared" them to behave. Simply, parents must learn through difficult episodes that they lost "control," if they ever possessed such control, of their children before they were born. We educators have much to do to gain admittance to decision making, or, as the poet Robert Frost noted, "we have miles to go," as we prepare for and participate in deliberations that will shape public schooling in future years.

Our preparation must include our practice of thinking clearly and speaking directly, specifically to other adults in our communities. We continue to prepare as we contribute to, even begin to participate in public dialogue about education. Who on our faculty speaks at public forums such as meetings of the Board of Trustees, of the City Council, of activist groups fostering increased civic support of public schooling, of meals for schoolchildren of poverty during the week-ends, of shelters for homeless adolescents, and of opportunities for students and families to become citizens? Who, indeed? And who writes regular columns for local newspapers about issues and circumstances related to the community's schools; or, even, occasional letters to editors about matters critical to the improvement of schooling? Who among us will write the first letter; the initial Op-Ed column? Who can we encourage to step up to this need? And, how strong is our commitment to support our colleagues who decide to enter the local public discourse about schooling?

And, how clearly do we think? Likely, we are less careful than we believe that we are. In my experience, as one example, most Americans, including most educators, routinely confuse cause and influence, a distinction that is critical to increased understanding of and communication about schooling. Attention to this problem illustrates some of the exceedingly disconcerting and serious problems attendant to careless thinking and the well-intentioned use of the meanings of cause and intention.

Note the following argument.

"To go fishing" is to express behaviorally an intention to fish, that is, seriously to hope to catch fish. To return from fishing without fish is a failure of intention *only* if the fisherperson did not truly intend to engage in efforts to fish; for example, to get away from the stresses of work or home for a few hours, to continue to place a baited hook into the water at the same unproductive place, not to change the hook and/or bait used at a particularly familiar spot along the river bank, not to be aware of the particularities of the fishing site such as depth of water, nature of the river or lake bank, temperature, wind conditions, and recent rains or runoffs from nearby fields. However, if the fisherperson employed much or all of his/her knowledge and skills of fishing and still caught no fish; he/she logically could claim that his/her fishing was accomplished inasmuch as he/she operationally attended to fish.

Moreover, even this logic is suspect without consideration of a significant factor in the intention and acts of fishing (deliberately trying to catch fish). That factor is the fish. That is, perhaps the fish in the river on a particular day were engaged in responses to a rainfall the night before or simply were interested in doing something other than looking at what ordinarily would be attractive bait jiggling in the water. Fish, to fulfill the "causal" or the "outcomes based" understanding of "fishing," simply must cease their normal behaviors, swiftly and without regard to other options, and swim with but one purpose to bite onto the fisherperson's hook. Were this the ordinary case, no fisherperson would leave the site of his/her fishing without as many fish as the times that he/she cast their baited hook. The fisherperson, as an intentional actor does not "cause" the fish to take the bait; they "intend" that the fish takes the bait, "hope" or "wish" that the fish darts at the bait with mouth wide open and, in taking the bait, the fish becomes hooked. Essential to a sound, logical conception of fishing are two essential notions: (a) that the fisherperson seriously intends and acts to engage in fishing; and (b) the fisherperson does not control the fish; rather, the fish "controls" itself. Assuredly, expert fisherpersons increase their probability of "catching fish" through their increased experience and motivation, with appropriate equipment, and their never-ending recognition of their need to "outwit" the fish.

Similarly, a business person does not grow a business; the business (i.e., with a mindful leader, an adequate workforce, active salespeople, and supportive business climate) develops or it goes bankrupt. A lumberman *does not* grow trees; trees grow. Attorneys *do not* win or lose lawsuits; their clients receive favorable or unfavorable judgments. Physicians *do not* heal a patient; the medications and procedures that physicians employ and/or prescribe to patients only *may* heal the patient. And, teachers teach, but their students are the ones who learn or do not learn.

Carefully note the circumstances and logic of these assertions. They contradict the common-sense "sayings" so familiar to most Americans and require us to abandon comfortable, if incorrect and utterly misleading, meanings.

Another example; a farmer *does not cause* a crop to make. To be sure, the farmer must till the soil, fertilize the soil if necessary, plant seeds at the appropriate time of year, and probably clear weeds away from the growing plants in the crop. But the farmer does not control the seed; the elements in the seed control it. As well, the farmer does not control the amount and frequency of rain, the temperature, the amount and intensity of sunlight, and not even animals that might break a hole in the fence surrounding the field to forage amidst the growing crop; and more.

To the extent that the farmers claim to have made the crop, they can only be logically incorrect and arrogantly self-serving. Moreover, farmers whose actions match their intentions to make a season's crop logically cannot be held accountable for what they cannot control (e.g., rainfall, drought), even though their losses may bankrupt their operations.

Thus, in education we must also be clear about how we speak and understand how intention to teach operates in educational practice. Without exception, to fulfill their role, teachers must sincerely want their students to learn something (e.g., a story, a concept, a skill, a process, definitions) and they must offer (teach) them (with) appropriate readings, remarks and instructions, and activities (exercises) as well as to make time available to them to use toward their learning, their achievement. Even as teachers *must* teach, students *may* or *may not* learn. Indeed, students' engagements with the teacher's intentions often begin with these students' intentions to engage or not to engage substantive content using exercises and activities offered by teachers. If students' intentions are sound and if they possess the necessary background knowledge and capabilities, they likely will learn— some bits or much—from the encounter with teaching. However, if they do *not* intend to learn or if their intentions are at a very low level and/or if they do not have adequate prerequisite knowledge or skills, and/or if their capabilities are well beneath those required by reasonable engagements with the subject matter, they likely will not learn or likely will learn little and that only at a superficial level.

In this conception, *teachers teach as intention*; teaching is *not* consequential. Also, learning is intentional. That is, for a teacher to have taught does not require that their students have learned. Teachers do not cause learning. Likewise, students' learning logically is intentional. They can and do learn much without a teacher's intervention. Teachers may influence students' learning, but they also may not influence it. Logically like the discussion of the fisherman's efforts previously noted, teachers must not be held accountable for what they cannot control. Students, as Harold Benjamin has insisted, are "under their own command." They must do their own learning, whether or not they are influenced by sensitive, alert, knowledgeable teachers. In the best of all possible worlds, all teachers intentionally and actively influence intentional and active students to learn the school offerings. But such a world is theoretic. We must remember, however, that our world is real and *not* theoretic. Part of our teaching must have to do with helping students realize that, for them to learn, they truly must intend (seriously want) to learn and must invest their talents and time toward that end.

Thinking clearly along these and similar lines and with the addition of effective communication with other adults in the community, educators reasonably should be able to advance the cause of solid, productive schooling. Advancement may be rapid; or it could be frustratingly slow; it probably will be slow. With clear and unambiguous intentions and actions to think clearly and to speak (and to write) responsibly, educators can claim intellectual respect as well as join policy development deliberations and become serious and meaningful actors in school improvement undertakings.

SCHOOLING FOR TOMORROW'S AMERICA IS DEVELOPED FOR THE HERE AND NOW, NOT FOR SOMEWHERE ELSE AND IN SOME UNKNOWN FUTURE

To be concerned about the nature of public schooling in the hard times of the present is an act of faith in the future. Some children in today's kindergartens will begin their own families before the end of the first quarter of the twenty-first century. At that same time, some pupils in middle schools during the current academic year will be receiving advanced degrees from graduate and professional schools. Groups in our society may blanche at such recognitions, but reality admits no other prospect. Accordingly, schooling for tomorrow must be recognized as schooling of today. Perceived in these terms, the future of America is developing before our eyes, in the here and now.

Political actions, particularly those by board members and legislators, which will impact American schools this year, will affect the quality of schooling engaged by students for years into the future. Continued rollbacks in appropriations for education, begun several years ago and forecast to increase routinely into the next decades, likely will eliminate already crippled school arts, music, and physical education programs. Funds simply will be unavailable to employ teachers in those specialty fields. Moreover, once absent from public schooling, the probability appears reasonable that politicians will judge the schools without these offerings as adequate or sound enough for the America of those (future) times. Consequently, schoolchildren of the present and foreseeable future reasonably could encounter a much poorer curriculum than was available to their parents.

On the other hand, such a doomsday analysis, surely a corruption of the ideals of American public schooling, should not even be thinkable. Certainly, it must not become realized. America's future deserves much better than for its people's education to be jeopardized by a doctrinaire politics that insists on drastic reduction or elimination of necessary governmental services to its citizens. In all likelihood, the politics of our times must undergo a substantial "gut-check" as soon as possible.

Does our society really want a radically diminished public schooling? If it does, it need only continue in the direction that its politics currently points. Or does it want an education that matches its finest aspirations? If this second direction is its choice, it must surmount the deadlocked partisanship that frustrates mindful consideration of any effort to reach a common ground. It will embrace proposals to make viable some or many options to swell the schooling opportunities for its young citizens. Furthermore, it will open its arms to a public schooling that will match our society's ideal of the importance of individual persons in community.

In order to liberate schooling, our society, at the appropriate governmental levels, will raise taxes to provide the funds necessary to develop rich programs of instruction, to assure strong and responsible educational offerings to a massive population with impressive differences, to emphasize modern electronic media at all levels of study as well as to encourage solid field studies in the community and laboratory investigations conducted at school. It will make available adequate funds with which to employ increasingly well-prepared teachers. It will abandon centralizing mandates and substitute invitations to education professionals to deliberate, to invent, and to act on their decisions. Its proper insistence on accountability must emphasize open access to the richness of public school offerings and interactions as well as fulsome disclosure of its operations. To be sure, ordinary test results should be available in a variety of public formats, but so also open for regular and serious review should be additional and even richer evidence such as genuine portfolios of students' achievements.

Such improved provisions for American public schooling cannot be expected in the near term. The hard times of the present continue to choke the prospects of a more robust public schooling. Our society, on the other hand, has been through hard times during earlier years. We know from our past that a much stronger and more accessible public schooling can be generated even during hard times and, especially, as hard times dissolve. Our generation of educators can be a part of the needed renaissance. Of course, we can.

ACKNOWLEDGMENT

Special thanks for extensive and very helpful comments upon earlier drafts are extended to Gerald A. Ponder, PhD; Matthew D. Davis, PhD; and O. Luke Davis, III, JD.

CHAPTER 2

EDUCATIONAL AIMS FOR THE TWENTY-FIRST CENTURY

Nel Noddings
Stanford University

Statements of educational aims for the twenty-first century show some worldwide similarities. Everywhere we see cooperation elevated above competition, critical thinking over masses of routine skills and information, and creativity over mastery of pre-specified material. Despite the near-universal statement of these aims, education in the United States is pushing doggedly for more standardization, higher test scores on information-laden tests, and ever greater emphasis on GPAs, SATS, and rankings. One might reasonably conclude that education in the United States is mired in twentieth century thinking.

Let us consider what we are doing with respect to these valuable aims.

COOPERATION

Just recently, President Obama told the American people that America needs to "out-build, out-innovate, and out-educate" the rest of the world. Why? The answer to that question seems to be that America must retain its

Schooling for Tomorrow's America, pages 21–29

position of world domination; to be "number one." To many of us, such thinking is patently dangerous. It is a prime example of twentieth century thinking, and that has to change. Even if we reject the idea of world government, we must still recognize that we are living in what should be considered a world community. In that setting, bragging and strutting are not conducive to warm community relations. Further, it seems unlikely that our own prosperity depends upon our beating and surpassing all others. Rather, we must begin to think in terms of working together toward peace and prosperity for everyone.

Our conception of generosity should probably change also. Instead of the *noblesse oblige* that has characterized our thinking in the past, we should think seriously about worldwide interdependence and working shoulder-to-shoulder with people who need help at one time and who will, in turn, help us when we have needs. In the next section, I will emphasize critical thinking, but we can also see the need for it here on this topic of cooperation and interdependence. We need to examine the role of religion, for example, in maintaining notions of charity, the "ever-present" poor, and stars in the crowns of those who give. The concept of entitlement also needs deeper analysis. Perhaps the concept most in need of critical thinking is *growth*. Instead of growth which invites competition, we need to think more in terms of *stability* and *sustainability*.

Unfortunately, our schools are working against a genuine program of cooperation. Although many schools have adopted the language of the twenty-first century aims including that of cooperation, they continue to promote a counter-productive spirit of competition within their walls. Why do they persist in computing and publishing class-rankings, for example? The whole enterprise seems schizophrenic. On the one hand, educators enthuse over the ideal of learning for its own sake; on the other, they encourage students to compete for the highest grades, and we know, from multiple studies, that this competition diverts attention away from engaged learning and toward whatever it takes to win in the game of rankings.

We exhibit another intellectual fault when we award extra credit for Advanced Placement (AP) courses. Why should students get more credit for taking such courses than their peers who may do excellent work in, say, machine shop? Reasonably, AP course work merits credit at the college level for passing college level courses; however, what justification is there for extra high school credit for these courses? Schools, as incubators of democracy, should promote a variety of excellences; they should not increase pernicious class and social differences.

Perhaps we should even reconsider keeping grade-point averages (GPAs). A personal note might be helpful here. I was valedictorian of my high school class (many years ago), but I have no idea what my GPA was or how the honor was decided. I do know that I did not have all A's (a nice sprinkling of A+'s, however) and that there were marking periods in which I was so captivated by one subject that I paid less attention to others. Must a good student give equal attention to every subject? That is the attitude we encourage when we make GPAs competitive.

But if we drop GPAs, extra credit for AP classes, class rankings, and perhaps even grades, how will we maintain standards? Think about it. On written work, we should make suggestions and ask students to "revise and resubmit." On mathematical concepts and skills, we should insist that they take re-tests on important topics they have not mastered before going on to the next unit of study. But, if we use such a procedure, one may object, the students will be strung out from unit three to unit ten! How can we manage this? That is a good question and one that we should work on creatively. The problem is manageable, but its solution requires cooperation, critical thinking, and creativity. The alternative is to give some students good grades, some bad grades, and ignore the fact that some are learning almost nothing.

The increased use of cooperative groups in our schools might be taken as evidence that the twenty-first century emphasis on cooperation is being taken seriously. But small groups are often urged to cooperate within the group so that their group can surpass and defeat other groups. The ultimate purpose of such small group work, then, is still successful competition.

An emphasis on cooperation does not imply total abandonment of competition. Indeed, some competition is healthy. For individuals, competition is healthy if it leads to better performances, if the activity continues to be enjoyable, and if one can take some pleasure in the success of opponents. For groups, competition is healthy if it leads to better products and performances and if it demonstrably contributes to the common good. The health of the Earth itself depends on the subordination of competition to cooperation.

CRITICAL THINKING

Critical thinking is named over and over as a crucial aim for twenty-first century education. In an increasingly complex world of information and technology where people must communicate across language and cultural differences, critical thinking might be thought of as a new basic skill. But, once again, we seem to be working against our own stated purpose. We say that we want to teach critical thinking, but we ignore the conditions required to teach it effectively, and we fail to use it in planning and evaluating our professional work.

If we are going to teach critical thinking, we must introduce and discuss critical issues (Noddings, 2006). There is little incentive to apply critical thinking to dull routines and memorization. But perhaps we can teach the skills required for critical thinking through a combination of formal and informal logic. There was great interest (and debate) on this possibility in the 1960s and 1970s. Some philosophers of education argued that we can teach the skills of observing, inferring, generalizing, stating assumptions, evaluating statements for accuracy, and detecting logical errors in isolation from any specific subject matter. Others argued that critical thinking requires familiarity—solid knowledge—of the field in which it is to be applied. The second group did not deny the need for skills named by the first group, but they insisted that such skills cannot be learned or applied effectively outside a domain of knowledge. (For a fuller discussion of these issues, see the chapter on critical thinking in Noddings, 2012b).

As educators, we should apply some critical thinking to the arguments about critical thinking. Reasonably, elements of formal and informal logic should be taught wherever they may be relevant to the subjects we teach. As a mathematics teacher, I always started my geometry classes with a unit on logic; later I included some symbolic logic in my philosophy classes. But, in doing so, I was in substantial agreement with those who see critical thinking as largely domain-bound. I think it was Michael Scriven who, some years ago, said that when we take an expert outside of his field of expertise, we can expect "instant irrationality." Perhaps that unhappy situation arises from too narrow and formal a conception of critical thinking.

An essential feature of critical thinking in everyday life and citizenship is *listening*, especially a willingness to listen to and evaluate fairly the ideas expressed by people outside our political, religious, or social group. In the United States today, there is a frightening incapacity for this sort of listening and thinking. Cass Sunstein (2009) has drawn our attention to "group polarization," a phenomenon in which people automatically agree with people in their own group and disagree with those in the "other" group. In such a situation, little or no critical thinking is applied by either group. The danger in such behavior is simple; it puts our democracy at risk.

To encourage critical thinking on social, political, and moral matters, we must introduce and discuss issues on which there are opposing views. Teachers charged with conducting such discussions must exercise pedagogical neutrality; that is, they must conscientiously present all reasonable arguments on all sides of an issue, preferably in the words of those espousing the views. Students should then apply the logical skills they have learned for assessing arguments, but—unfortunately—the skills of formal logic will rarely settle disputes involving values. The search must go on for points of agreement or, in many cases, a decision must be made to drop an irresolvable point and commit ourselves to working together on other projects. The attitude exhibited by teachers in discussing controversial topics is expressed in a comment I used in most of my classes: "Reasonable people may differ on this." Students came to anticipate this line and would sometimes pre-empt me by saying it themselves to cool down a disagreement. Notice that this attitude goes well beyond the skills of formal logic but is of crucial importance in both critical thinking and democratic relationships.

One of the loveliest examples of this sort of critical thinking is illustrated in a book by E.O. Wilson, *The Creation* (2006). The book is cast as a letter from Wilson, a secular humanist, to a southern Baptist preacher. There is no hope that they will agree on basic matters of religion. After outlining their irresolvable differences, Wilson asks, "Does this difference in worldview separate us in all things?" He goes on to write, "I suggest that we set aside our differences in order to save the Creation" (Wilson, 2006, p. 4). Wilson believes that they share a deep commitment to the well-being of the Earth and that they will find a way to work together on related projects—perhaps for very different reasons. This is a part of critical thinking too often over-looked. It asks us to look beyond differences to common commitments. It is not aimed at demonstrating who is right on a particular issue but, rather, how both sides can work on *something* for the common good. It involves a commitment to mutual respect and sensitivity to inevitable disagreement.

A basic purpose of critical thinking at the high school level is to help students understand themselves and the predicaments they will eventually encounter. Consider one crucial example. We rarely give young people an opportunity to think critically about what may happen to them if they join the military right out of high school. Their classmates who move on to study the humanities at colleges of liberal arts will be introduced to great literature and political history that will encourage them to think deeply about what sometimes happens to the moral identity of warriors. The young people who bear the burden of combat know that they may suffer physical injury and perhaps psychological trauma from what they undergo, but they rarely hear anything about the lasting trauma inflicted by the loss of moral identity. What happens to young warriors when they cannot come to grips with what they have done in the stressful situation of war? (Shay, 1994) surely we owe it to our young people to discuss such matters in an honest, balanced way (Noddings, 2012a).

If teachers are to promote and guide critical thinking, they must themselves be capable critical thinkers. In particular, they should be able to apply critical thinking to the enterprise of teaching. Today's teachers are too often told exactly what to do and with one major aim—to increase test scores. The emphasis among policymakers is to find and employ methods and structures that will "scale"; that is, to find procedures that will work everywhere for all students. John Dewey warned us almost a century ago about the foolishness of such a quest for certainty. Instead of embracing an idea whole hog or rejecting it entirely, critical thinkers should ask critical questions on suggested methods: When might this be useful; under what conditions; for which students; for what purpose? Might it accomplish one of our aims but undermine an even more important one?

Think of all the wonderful ideas that have appeared (and disappeared) over the years in educational theory: discovery; intuition, mastery learning, task analysis, object lessons, role playing, behavioral objectives, group work, Socratic questioning, spaced practice, guided fantasy, mnemonic devices, wait time, drill, stage theories, incidental learning, ability grouping, lecture method, open education, learning to learn, audio-visual aids, activity methods, readiness, teacher-centered instruction, whole word and/or phonics, online learning, student-centered lessons, overt thinking, spiral curriculum...

The job of critical thinkers is not to look over this list and decide which idea will dominate their approach to teaching. The task is to explore each idea critically and ask the sort of questions suggested above. These are the questions that teachers and supervisors sould explore together. Good supervisors do not tell teachers what to do. They ask teachers to discuss what they are doing and why. They make occasional suggestions and back these with reasoned arguments tentatively held. Supervisors, too, should be critical thinkers.

CREATIVITY

In the twentieth century, the United States had an enviable talent for technological creativity. It also had a somewhat loosely structured system of secondary education, one that allowed considerable choice and some free time for tinkering and dreaming. American education contrasted sharply with the test-driven curricula favored in Asian Schools. Today, in a conscious effort to promote creativity, Chinese and Japanese schools are moving away from test-driven curricula, and American schools—giving lip-service to creativity as an educational aim—are moving steadily toward standardized test-driven curricula.

When what is to be learned is tightly prescribed in detail, there is little incentive to engage in creative exploration. An individual who indulges in such exploration may lose points on a test, while others gain points by sticking closely to exactly what is required. In mathematics classes, when a problem is solved, how often does the teacher ask students to explore— perhaps to invent—other ways to solve the problem? If the answer to this is one I hear frequently—that there is no time for this sort of thing—then I would point out even more forcefully that we are on the wrong track, busily undermining aims that should guide us.

Do our students have time for daydreaming, or is this habit of the mind totally forbidden? A whole world of reflection and productive thought has been generated by what started out as daydreaming, but we rarely even discuss the phenomenon in our schools. Instead, we concentrate on something called "time on task." In the last section, I provided a substantial list of ideas that have emerged in educational thought, and I advised that teacher should analyze them and put them to good use. I did not include "time on task" because I believe it has done more harm than good and because it is seriously misleading. How do we know, really, whether or not a student is "on task"? If a student is staring out the window, she may be thinking seriously about prime numbers. If the student next to her has his head inclined steadily at the worksheet in front of him, is he "on task"? He may be having erotic daydreams.

At least, we might discuss daydreaming with our students—how it is used to escape boredom, how it gives pleasure, and how it is sometimes the prelude to real creativity. E. V. Walter has reminded us, "The major unacknowledged activity in classrooms and factories, then, is daydreaming" (1988, p. 205). And Gaston Bachelard wrote that "the values that belong to daydreaming mark humanity in its depths…" (1964, p. 6). I am not suggesting that we encourage daydreaming in our classrooms but, rather, that we help students to consider the habit and evaluate what it contributes to their own pleasure and productivity.

We get in our own way again when we insist that creative work is, by its very nature, highly individualistic. Certainly its products often bear the unique marks of their creator. But we are learning more and more about the collaborative roots of creation. Vera John-Steiner (2000) has provided us with a stunning account of creative collaborations in art, science, music, mathematics, and literature. The collaboration is sometimes direct—people working together on a project—but often indirect, a whole network of conversation that supports the work of individual creators. One message for educators is to encourage students to talk to one another, share references, and build on one another's experience. A second message is for teachers to do the same. We can learn much from one another. Collaboration and creativity are synergistic.

I do not believe that all, or even many, students will be creative in all (or any) of the subjects we teach. This notion—that all students are potentially creative—is another of those all-or-nothing illusions. But all students should have opportunities to exercise whatever creative capabilities they possess. These opportunities should be made available in all of our courses—machine shop, photography, history—and the products of that creativity should be recognized.

Children are most likely to show some creative talent in one of the arts—drawing, acting, singing, playing an instrument, and making things. Indeed, I have known students who remained in high school just for art class or band. Some of them put up with my mathematics class because I admired their art and understood what it meant to them. Without these creative incentives, they would have dropped out. Elementary school teachers have watched academically slow students come alive when they have a chance to build stage scenery or work with classmates to design a mural. And how lovely it is to hear a roomful of youngsters sing together! Children love poetry, too, and respond to it with their whole bodies—chanting, dancing, crouching, pointing, growling, laughing. Have you ever seen a child younger than ten who did not like poetry? How many retain that love through high school?

Once again, we are working against our professed aims. We include creativity in our written statement of aims, and then we cut the arts to make more time for routine material that will appear on tests.

CONCLUSION

If we are serious about the twenty-first century aims we profess, we have to stand courageously against the "reform" movement that has oppressed education for almost three decades. The reformers are right to insist that we provide a good education for all of our children and that we work to reduce the achievement gap between races. But they are tragically wrong to put such emphasis on pre-specified, standardized curriculum and the results of tests used to measure proficiency on the skills and facts contained in that curriculum. We keep talking about hard work and its expected payoff and so justify heaps of homework. What about the joy of learning, the wonderful fun of figuring things out? Are there no intrinsic rewards in learning?

Reflect on the contradictions I have discussed here. We include *cooperation* as a primary aim for twenty-first century education, and then we increase our emphasis on GPAs, test scores, and class rankings. Competition, artificially and deliberately supported, undermines efforts at cooperation.

Critical thinking and problem solving are announced as newly important aims for education. But then we design our curricula to be standard—the same for everyone, everywhere—to align with tests that discourage original thinking. Students are stuffed with names, routine skills, problems-by-type, and material that carefully avoids controversy. They have no time for reflection or deep engagement with real problems. Even teachers—those who are supposed to teach critical thinking—are discouraged from actively challenging the increasingly scripted nature of their daily work.

We espouse creativity and then do our best to squelch it by forcing the same, pre-specified material on all students, overloading them with homework, and reducing their time with the arts.

Perhaps we should just abandon such lofty aims as cooperation, critical thinking, and simply state honestly our one great aim: to raise test scores. Sad.

REFERENCES

Bachelard, G. (1964). *The poetics of space* (M. Jolas, Trans.) New York: Orion Press.

John-Steiner, V. (2000). *Creative collaboration.* Oxford: Oxford University Press.

Noddings, N. (2006). *Critical lessons: What our schools should teach.* Cambridge: Cambridge University Press.

Noddings, N. (2012a). *Peace studies: How we come to love and hate war.* Cambridge: Cambridge University Press.

Noddings, N. (2012b). *Philosophy of education* (3rd ed.) Boulder, CO: Westview Press.

Shay, J. (1994). *Achilles in Vietnam: Combat trauma and the undoing of character.* New York: Scribner.

Sunstein, C. R. (2009). *Going to extremes: How like minds unite and divide.* New York: Oxford University Press.

Walter, E. V. (1988). *Placeways: A theory of the human environment.* Chapel Hill: University of North Caroline Press.

Wilson, E. O. (2006). *The creation: An appeal to save life on earth.* New York: W.W. Norton.

CHAPTER 3

TEACHER LEARNING AND LEADERSHIP

Community, Collaboration, and Challenge

Ann Lieberman
Stanford University

As a sixth grade teacher many years ago, I knew that as teachers we were learning a variety of information about students, relevance, content, engagement, moral dilemmas in the classroom and more. But it seemed that no one was interested in what we had to say. And I wondered what it would take to create the conditions where teachers could participate with the larger educational community about knowledge created in the classroom by us. Little did I know that I would have opportunities as a professor to teach, facilitate, study, organize and make possible teachers writing about their work.

During the last decade I have studied, or been involved in some way with, four different programs that get at the kinds of organizing conditions and the types of involvement that teach us how, and under what conditions, teachers' learning and leadership can be developed and mined. In each case, challenges of learning from the outside often conflict with learning on the inside; or learning a new role challenges the existing teacher culture; or dealing

Schooling for Tomorrow's America, pages 31–42
Copyright © 2014 by Information Age Publishing
All rights of reproduction in any form reserved.

with conflict while maintaining commitment to new ideas stalls the process of change. Yet, each case shows how community and collaboration can be developed, nurtured, and instructive in teaching us how to get at teacher learning and the development of teacher leadership. A central learning is that changing the teaching culture often leads to challenging the bureaucratic ways that schools are organized, particularly when professional ideas come in conflict with the existing norms of the organization (Talbert, 2010).

I start with the oldest professional development project in the United States which has been operating as a national network for over 30 years— The National Writing Project (NWP). It is important to note that community and collaboration in the NWP is built away from one's school at a school/university partnership and the challenge becomes how to bring the learning back home to one's school.

THE NATIONAL WRITING PROJECT: DEVELOPING LEARNING AND LEADERSHIP

From 1998 to 2000, and then another few years more, Diane Wood and I studied the National Writing Project (NWP), arguably the most successful professional development program in the United States. But as we were to learn, it was in no way typical of the professional development that either of us had experienced as teachers. Started by Jim Gray, a secondary English teacher, the NWP brings together a group of about 20 teachers on a university campus to participate in a professional development experience that can be anywhere from 3 to 5 weeks in duration called the *summer institute.* We studied two sites (among over 200) wanting to know why teachers said "The writing project changed my life" or "It gave me a community of teachers who cared passionately about constantly improving their practice." Everyone we talked with said that we should study the summer institute "because it is like magic." So, Diane Wood went to Oklahoma to study a rural site that was relatively new, housed at Oklahoma State University in Stillwater, and I went to Los Angeles to study an older urban site housed at the University of California at Los Angeles (UCLA; Lieberman & Wood, 2003).

Our study conducted over a two year period had three primary purposes:

- How, and in what ways, does the summer institute facilitate teacher learning and leadership in the context of a professional community?
- What seem to be the key attributes of the sites, and how do they try to provide for the social and intellectual learning as well as the building of community?
- How does each site create its own network arrangements for ongoing support beyond the summer institute?

We both went to the summer institutes in our respective sites and wrote down everything that was happening. We both observed and informally interviewed everyone we could find. It took us almost a year to figure out what was going on there and why this was an important example of the development of a community, opening up teachers to collaborate with one another, and creating the conditions for deep teacher learning and leadership. What we found was that there was a set of social practices that occurred during the institutes that seemed to develop a community; opened teachers up to the power of collaborating and learning from one another by its activities; and for some convinced them that they could be professional developers of other teachers.

The social practices included

- approaching each colleague as a potentially valuable contributor.
- honoring teacher knowledge;
- creating public forums for teacher sharing, dialogue, and critique;
- turning ownership over to the learners;
- situating human learning in practice and relationships;
- providing multiple entry points into the learning community;
- guiding reflection on teaching through reflection on learning;
- sharing leadership;
- promoting a stance of inquiry; and
- encouraging a re-conceptualization of professional identity and linking it to professional community.

These practices we came to understand were interactive and mutually dependent and that, together, generated a teacher culture that was highly collaborative. Integration and persistence to stick with these practices seemed to us to make an authentic professional learning community. No one ever told these teachers that everything that was happening to them as learners could be used in some way with their students. Yet, it turned out that this was professional development at its finest. Teachers became learners as participants taught their best strategy or lesson to the group and everyone went home with a fistful of ideas, many of which they could hone and shape to their own classrooms.

THE SUMMER INSTITUTE

These summer institutes each asked teachers to teach a favorite lesson or strategy (honoring teacher knowledge), be in a writing group (a public forum) and not only get feedback from their group, but present several times to the larger group (sharing leadership). Teachers started with what they knew and then opened up to reading research together and critiquing it, sharing literature and books that they had used and were effective with their students; and learning from one another in numerous ways (situating human learning in practice and relationships). A number of people became excited about teaching adults and were asked to be professional developers in their district. Needless to say, we were both excited to see and finally understand what it would take to build the kind of conditions that would encourage teachers' learning, and even open some teachers up to the possibilities of taking leadership (encouraging a re-conceptualization of professional identity).

Analyzing the NWP encouraged us to not only write a book but to understand the real possibilities of teachers learning from one another; becoming more articulate about their practice; and creating the organizational conditions for teachers to learn leadership. This was to start me on a mission to further understand the organizational conditions for teacher learning and led me to Toronto where I was to learn yet another type of collaboration, The Teacher Learning and Leadership Program (TLLP).

TEACHER LEARNING AND LEADERSHIP PROGRAM

In 2005, a newly elected Minister of Education in Toronto called together a Working Table on Teacher Development. This government recognized the need to bring together all stakeholders if they were going to truly change and enhance education in Ontario, after a fractious eight years of poor relationships with teachers. Those invited to the Working Table included the Ontario Teachers Federation (OTF) and its affiliates. This group was given the responsibility to make recommendations on effective supports for the professional learning of teachers. The Ministry of Education and the OTF worked together for two years trying to find out what was known in the literature and in practice that would help them design a new system of teacher development. Together, they decided that professional development needed to ensure a positive impact on students as well as teachers and that it include the development of teachers as leaders as well as learners (Lieberman, 2010).

They developed the following characteristics for professional learning which they felt needed to be

- coherent built on respect, responsibility, and results;
- attentive to adult learning styles;
- goal oriented and connected to improved student learning;
- built on evidence–informed research;
- encouraging of peer leadership;
- team or partner oriented, if possible; and
- oriented toward choice to accommodate teacher differences.

DEVELOPING A PROPOSAL

Teacher Learning and Leadership was born and the details were made known to teachers all over Ontario and beyond. A short application was designed for teachers to be sent for consideration of their proposed work. The proposal needed to have the name and summary of the project; how the project addresses participants" professional learning; how the project outcomes contribute to student learning: and the experience that teachers bring to their particular project. In another section, teachers needed to describe their goals, activities, and budget and how they would measure the outcomes of their project. The range of monetary support continues to be $1,000 to about $10,000 with a few going well beyond this as the teachers are encouraged to expand their project to other schools, networks and regions. Teachers receive the money after being chosen. So far, 93% of the projects involve teachers engaging in professional development in their own schools; 91% include other schools in the district; and 43% include other groups (e.g., conferences, websites, and publications).

When a cohort has been chosen, a conference is held to give support to the teachers; to clarify any questions, to make real the collaboration between Ministry and Federation; and to offer a variety of sessions that include

- developing and delivering a dynamic workshop;
- working with your team: facilitation skills;
- promoting your project: Persuasion not pontification; and
- sharing TLLP learning through technology (Introductory and Advanced).

TYPES OF TEACHER DEVELOPMENT PROJECTS

Looking inside some of the projects provides an interesting picture of what teachers choose to work on as well as the depth and breadth of what is possible when teachers are given a voice and choice of how to organize professional development that connects to their needs, contexts, interests, and strengths. The projects range from: Teachers with Technology— Engaging Readers with E-books to HIP: High Interest Programs that are multi-disciplinary in an attempt to create project based programs with "real world" value. There are projects on mathematics, music, language arts, science, social studies and more as well as some teacher made ideas like the "Success Room" for seventh and eighth graders who are having some kind of difficulty. Students learn to work with their peers and teachers until all find success.

WORKING AND LEARNING TOGETHER

Working with a fourth cohort (about 70 teachers and their team members), 85% of the teachers who get grants work with another teacher or a team of teachers. The TLLP program gives us an interesting example of what can happen when teachers are given an opportunity to propose professional development based on what they want to learn and need to learn, and at the same time it gives them an opportunity to take leadership with their peers and beyond, creating a collaborative setting. At the conferences where all successful proposers come, teachers learn that they are part of a larger professional learning community and many, for the first time, realize that teacher learning can be organized by collaborating with policy makers who believe in enabling teacher participation in their own and others' learning. Midway through the year, teachers come to a network meeting where they display what they have been doing and teachers learn, once again, the interesting work of their peers. Collaboration and community replace the normal compliance modes that have been a part of professional development programs for years. Challenges sometimes include the difficulties of getting other teachers involved, accepting the fact that their colleagues are the developers, not someone from outside the school.

This program provides us with a robust example of how practice, research, and enabling policy (Darling–Hammond & McLaughlin,1995) can change teaching, learning, and leading for both adults and their students.

These examples begin to teach us that teachers' learning can be organized in different ways providing choice, autonomy, collaboration and a larger professional community to replace the continued isolation of teachers. But, there are other examples of the development of teacher leadership where learning and leading take place as part of the development of a new role—a mentor for novice teachers.

MENTORING TEACHERS: THE NEW TEACHER CENTER WAY

Over 14 years ago, a young, bilingual elementary teacher who was visited by student teachers from U.C. Santa Cruz, Ellen Moir, was invited to the university to work with teacher educators to help build a more solid base for new teachers. This was the beginning of the birth of The New Teacher Center (NTC) which focused on creating a program for mentoring new teachers during their first two years of teaching now known as induction. The big idea was to select expert teachers who would become teacher leaders whose expertise would be in helping novice teachers be supported as they learn to teach. Their job would be to build on the novice teachers existing knowledge and help develop it so they would become more competent in their teaching. Novices who get support and become more effective are those that stay in teaching and continue learning.

STUDYING HOW MENTORS DEVELOP

For four years, in two different places where there were mentors available for new teachers, a researcher from the NTC (Susan Hanson) interviewed mentors to find out how they developed their skills and abilities in mentoring new teachers. Several of us were invited to work with Susan to see what we could learn from the rich data of these interviews as mentors learned to become leaders in their districts. What we learned was how these mentors negotiated a series of tensions that were inevitable as they went into different schools working with mentors. Negotiating these tensions taught these mentors a new role and helped fashion their leadership knowledge.

NAVIGATING THE REAL WORLD TENSIONS

We found that as mentors gain experience working in a variety of schools with different administrators and teachers, that mentors acquire new insights and new conceptions of themselves as leaders. They learn "how to be" as well as "how to work" in different school cultures. And they learn to navigate through a thicket of tensions which help them grow into their role as mentor leaders (Lieberman, Hanson, & Gless, 2011).

THE TENSIONS OF MENTORING

We found five tensions that seemed to occur as mentors found themselves in many different school cultures dealing with veteran teachers and their principals. Eventually, these tensions became a part of the job and a part of what it means to become a mentor. But, they also turned out to be important means for mentors to learn the complexities of the role. These tensions turned out to involve

- building a new identity,
- developing trusting relationships with different members of the school culture,
- accelerating teacher development,
- mentoring in challenging contexts, and
- learning leadership in the mentoring context.

Having been chosen to be mentors because of their excellence in teaching, mentors quickly find themselves struggling with who they are, what their work really is, and how to feel confident in their new identity. They knew what to do in their classrooms, but now they have to deal with the dynamics of not one, but several different school cultures, principals with different leadership styles and expectations, veteran teachers, as well as their mentees.

Mentors must also learn to establish a relationship, not only with the mentee, but with the veteran teachers and other adults in the school. Somehow, the mentor must find a way to be a broker, facilitator, sometimes protector, or even an advocate. And, these roles shift and change dependent on the different actors in the school culture.

Some mentors work in schools that are dysfunctional in a number of ways and they need to help support the mentees despite the difficulties. Other times mentors who have been elementary teachers find themselves mentoring in secondary schools where the culture and the leadership team are totally different than what they have learned. Sometimes, there is a lack of resources, or difficult working conditions and the mentor must learn how to navigate the relationships and tough contexts while providing support for their mentee.

Perhaps at the heart of mentoring (and learning), is how mentors accelerate growth in their mentee. How do you build a trusting relationship with mentees as well as facilitate their continuous learning about teaching? Mentees differ. Some are open and friendly. Some are protective or shy. Some feel overburdened and embarrassed by their inability to keep students engaged in learning. In all cases, the negotiations demand sensitivity, flexibility, reflection, support, and as much intelligence as one can muster.

Most mentors would not call themselves leaders, yet working through all these difficult circumstances and human relationships, mentors learn what it takes to lead. Some learn to be change agents when the situation demands that a wrong be righted. Others learn to become good at brokering difficult situations. Mentors learn to organize; not only their own work, but skillfully helping the mentees to do the same. In learning how to handle different cultures and personalities, mentors become adept at negotiating the tensions that inevitably arise. The struggles to negotiate difficult situations are ubiquitous in schools and these experiences help them develop a leadership stance as well as the confidence to build the capacity of their mentees. Although mentors become leaders as they learn to work in a variety of schools with numerous administrators and teachers, some professional development programs deliberately groom teachers for leadership as we see, once again, how this happens in the NWP.

How Teachers Become Leaders in the NWP

To find out how teachers learn to lead as well as the problems they face, we called together 31 educators who had started out as teachers, and now held some leadership position (Lieberman & Friedrich, 2010). We invited them to a two day retreat sponsored by the NWP as well as a follow up of two more days four months later, hoping that we could support them to write vignettes describing a piece of their leadership experience, with an emphasis on their learning. Previously, Miles, Saxl, and Lieberman (1988) had studied "change agents" in New York and had learned to help participants bound their stories by a common set of questions (and prompts) helping them to write a vignette. We set out to acquire a set of vignettes hoping to reveal both the dynamic practices that these leaders use as individuals as well as some common themes across their narratives.

We worked in groups providing support for their writing and subsequent revisions. We explained that we were doing a study of leadership work in the NWP and that we were looking for the content of their work; how they developed as leaders; how they got support; and the tensions they negotiated along the way. We encouraged the participants to write about their leadership by selecting a series of activities—less than a full blown case—but more than one event—that "showed" rather than "told" how they were learning to lead. We asked them to describe:

- What you were hoping would happen or be accomplished?
- What is the context within which the work occurred?
- What was involved?
- What was the impact of the work?
- Why do you think it happened?
- What role did you play?
- What feels most important about this work?

During the four months between the first and second retreats, we each worked with our group members on their revisions. At the second retreat, group members read their vignettes and got feedback and revised once more. Looking across all the vignettes a small number of themes were identified. They included: acquiring an identity; learning to build collegiality and community; learning to make conflict productive; and reflecting on old and new knowledge.

ACQUIRING AN IDENTITY

The vignettes revealed a number of ways that the participants felt that they were becoming more comfortable with their leadership roles. One teacher wrote about how she moved from a Department Chair to an assistant principal and had to work through the snubbing that the teachers gave her as she joined "the dark side." The same people who loved her as Department Chair, accused her "not being a teacher" and, therefore, unworthy of teaching them anything. Another teacher got a job in a university and struggled with the idea that she might not be any good and people would not listen to her. After all, she was a good classroom teacher, but would it apply to higher education students?

LEARNING TO BUILD COLLEGIALITY AND COMMUNITY

Another teacher who had been a consultant in a secondary school was appointed as an assistant principal. She had learned to facilitate teacher learning by "working alongside" the teachers. She found that she must distinguish between some "principal like" expectations as well as those which will allow her to build community. Another teacher wrote about how he could provide leadership in other schools, but found it difficult to do in his own school. After seven years had passed, he applied for and got a Title I position and finally realized that he is capable of helping, teaching and improving other teachers' skills and abilities in his own school.

LEARNING TO MAKE CONFLICT PRODUCTIVE

Several vignettes describe how conflict arises and how they negotiate forward looking solutions. In one vignette, a social studies teacher, who does professional development one day a week, describes how she was working with a number of colleagues helping them learn how to use writing in their classes. This had been the focus of the district. The district then decided to shift to a focus on test preparation. The teacher, feeling that the teachers who she was involved with were making great strides in their literacy learning, decided to keep it going and even invited a district person to come and observe. Although she was going against the district's new initiatives, she felt that what she was doing was far more useful to teachers and their students. She decided to invite the district person who was coordinating the new effort to her school. As he saw what the teachers were doing, he encouraged her to keep on with what she had been doing in lieu of test prep. The potential conflict was ameliorated by the teacher's learning and her courageous leadership.

REFLECTING ON NEW AND OLD KNOWLEDGE: LEARNING FROM PRACTICE

Teacher leaders realized that they knew a great deal about pedagogy as that is why they had been chosen. But, they soon came to understand that there was so much more to learn, about the schools they worked in, the different ways one needed to approach adult learning; framing leading as a problem of teaching; and realizing that they could weave together multiple sources of knowledge—their own and all that they were learning about school cultures and how to improve them.

WHAT LESSONS CAN WE LEARN FROM THESE EXAMPLES?

There are a number of lessons that can be learned by looking across these four successful programs for teachers. They all provide for

- learning in a group,
- teaching each other what they have learned,
- working on problems as teachers define them,
- developing collaborative structures for learning,
- navigating the inevitable tensions of change,
- teaching teachers how to approach their colleagues,
- building commitment for organizing teachers as leaders,
- learning outside the school and bringing it inside, and
- enabling policies that support teacher learning and leadership.

Although teachers have incurred increased restrictions on their teaching and rules of all kinds that narrow what school is about in the United States, these programs described above attempt to support teachers and their learning and build leadership in both pre-service as well as professional development. If we are to have a future for public schools and do serious work on transforming our schools to deal with twenty-first century skills and abilities, we need to look at evidence in our own country, as well as in Europe and Asia. We see that teachers need to be involved in studying their own learning as they work in collaboration with others (Darling-Hammond & Lieberman, 2012). We are just beginning to understand the kinds of conditions that must be organized for teachers to go public with their work. We know that building professional communities inside and outside the school provides the kind of environment where teachers open up to expanding their repertoire. They learn from others, and with support, also take responsibility for leadership. These are the kind of lessons that will help us build a better future for schools, teachers, and students and will teach us how to create the necessary conditions for teacher learning and leadership.

REFERENCES

Darling-Hammond, L., & McLaughlin, M. W. (1995). Policies that support professional development in an era of reform. *Phi Delta Kappan, 76.* pp.

Darling-Hammond, L., & Lieberman, A. (2012). *Teacher education around the world: Changing policies and practices.* London, UK: Routledge.

Talbert, J. (2010). *Professional learning communities at the crossroads: How systems hinder or engender change. The second handbook of educational change,* Part 2 (pp. 555–571). Springer: Dordrecht.

Lieberman, A., & Wood, D. (2003). *Inside the national writing project: Connecting network learning and classroom teaching.* New York: Teachers College Press.

Lieberman, A. (2010, Summer) Teachers, learners, leaders: Joining practice, policy and research. *Educational Leadership online, 67,* June 15.

Lieberman, A., Hanson, S., & Gless, J. (2011). *Mentoring teachers: Navigating the real world tensions.* San Francisco, CA: Jossey-Bass.

Lieberman, A., & Friedrich, L. (2010). *How teachers become leaders: Learning from practice and research.* San Francisco, CA: Jossey-Bass.

Miles, M. B., Saxl, E., & Lieberman, A. (1988). What skills do educational "change agents" need? An empirical view. *Curriculum Inquiry, 18*(2), 157–193.

CHAPTER 4

EDUCATING CITIZENS FOR TOMORROW'S DIVERSE WORLD

James A. Banks
University of Washington, Seattle

I was an elementary school student in the Arkansas delta in the 1950s. One of my most powerful memories is the image of the happy and loyal slaves in my social studies textbooks. I also remember that there were three other Blacks in my textbooks: Booker T. Washington, the educator; George Washington Carver, the scientist; and Marian Anderson, the contralto. I had several persistent questions throughout my school days: Why were the slaves pictured as happy? Were there other Blacks in history beside the two Washingtons and Anderson? Who created this image of slaves? Why? The image of the happy slaves was inconsistent with everything I knew about the African American descendants of enslaved people in my segregated community. We had to drink water from fountains labeled "colored," and we could not use the city's public library. However, we were not happy about either of these legal requirements. In fact, we resisted these laws in powerful but subtle ways each day. As children, we savored the taste of "White wa-

Schooling for Tomorrow's America, pages 43–64
Copyright © 2014 by Information Age Publishing
All rights of reproduction in any form reserved.

ter" when the authorities were preoccupied with more serious infractions against the racial caste system.

AN EPISTEMOLOGICAL JOURNEY

Throughout my schooling, these questions remained cogent as I tried to reconcile the representations of African Americans in textbooks with the people I knew in my family and community. I wanted to know why these images were highly divergent. My undergraduate curriculum did not help answer my questions. I read one essay by a person of color during my four years in college, *Stranger in the Village* by James Baldwin (1953/1985). In this powerful essay, Baldwin describes how he was treated as the "Other" in a Swiss village. He was hurt and disappointed—not happy—about his treatment.

My epistemological quest to find out why the slaves were represented as happy became a lifelong journey that continues, and the closer I think I am to the answer, the more difficult and complex both my question and the answers become. The question—Why were the slaves represented as happy?—has taken different forms in various periods of my life. I have lived with these questions all of my professional life. *I now believe that the biographical journeys of researchers greatly influence their values, their research questions, and the knowledge they construct.* The knowledge they construct mirrors their life experiences and values. The happy slaves in my school textbooks were invented by the Southern historian Ulrich B. Phillips (1918/1966). The images of enslaved people he constructed reflected his belief in the inferiority of African Americans and his socialization in Georgia near the turn of the century (Smith & Inscoe, 1993).

THE VALUES OF RESEARCHERS

Social scientists are human beings who have both minds and hearts. However, their minds and the products of their minds have dominated research discourse in history and the social sciences. The hearts of social scientists exercise a cogent influence on research questions, findings, concepts, generalizations, and theories. I am using "heart" as a metaphor for values, which are the beliefs, commitments, and generalized principles to which social scientists have strong attachments and commitments. The value dimensions of social science research was largely muted and silenced in the academic community and within the popular culture until the neutrality of the social sciences was strongly challenged by the postmodern, women's studies, and ethnic studies movements of the 1960s and 1970s (King, 1995; Ladner, 1973; Rosenau, 1992).

Social science research has supported historically and still supports educational policies that affect the life chances and educational opportunities of students. The educational policies supported by mainstream social science and educational researchers have often harmed low-income students and students of color. However, the values of social scientists are complex within diverse nations such as the United States, Canada, and the United Kingdom. Social science and educational research over time and often within the same period have both reinforced inequality (Herrnstein & Murray, 1994) and supported liberation and human betterment (Clark, 1965).

In my American Educational Research Association (AERA) Presidential address (Banks, 1998), I describe research that supports these claims:

- The cultural communities in which individuals are socialized are also epistemological communities that have shared beliefs, perspectives, and knowledge.
- Social science and historical research are influenced in complex ways by the life experiences, values, personal biographies, and epistemological communities of researchers.
- Knowledge created by social scientists, historians, and public intellectuals reflect and perpetuate their epistemological communities, experiences, goals, and interests.
- How individual social scientists interpret their cultural experiences is mediated by the interaction of a complex set of status variables, such as gender, social class, age, political affiliation, religion, and region. (p. 5)

VALUATION AND KNOWLEDGE CONSTRUCTION

In nations around the world, the assimilationist ideology has been the dominant historical force since the age of colonization and the expansion of Western nations into the Americas, the Caribbean, Africa, Asia, and Australia. The assimilationist ideology maintains that in order to construct a cohesive nation and civic culture individuals from diverse racial, ethnic, cultural, linguistic, and religious groups must surrender their home and community cultures and acquire those of the dominant and mainstream groups (Patterson, 1977; Schlesinger, 1991). Assimilationists believe that ethnic attachments prevent individuals from developing commitments and allegiance to the national civic culture (see Kymlicka, 2004, for a critique of this view).

The assimilationist ideology was seriously challenged by the ethnic re-vitalization and protest movements of the 1960s, 1970s, and 1980s. These movements began with and were stimulated by the Black civil rights move-ment in the United States (Painter, 2006). Multiculturalism and multi-cultural education grew out of these movements. Multiculturalism chal-lenges and questions the assimilationist ideology and argues that ethnic and cultural diversity enriches the mainstream culture, that the identities of individuals are "multiple, nested, and overlapping" (Kymlicka, 2004 p. xiv), and that individuals who are firmly rooted in their home and com-munity cultures are more—not less—capable of being effective citizens of the nation-state and cosmopolitan citizens of the world community (Ap-piah, 2006).

During the 1990s and 2000s, the assimilationist ideology, neoliberalism, and conservatism became robust in Western nations. A number of factors contributed to the resurgence of neoliberalism and conservatism, both of which support assimilationism. These factors included increased migration around the world and the xenophobia that arose in response to it, the world economic crisis, and security concerns caused by the coordinated bombings in the United States on September 11, 2001, and other bombings around the world linked to the actions of Muslim fundamentalists (d'Appollonia & Reich, 2008). These bombings included the four commuter trains in Ma-drid, Spain on March 11, 2004; the bombings in the London transportation system on July 7, 2005; and the bombing of a Red Sea resort at Sharm el-Sheikh in Egypt on July 23, 2005.

The rise of neoliberalism and the resurgence of assimilationism in West-ern Europe in nations such as The Netherlands and France were mani-fested in the xenophobia directed against Muslims, the controversy over the wearing of the headscarve (hijab) in France (Bowen, 2007; Scott, 2007), and the statement made by French president Nicolas Sarkozy about the wearing of the burka. In a speech on June 22, 2009, he said, "The burka is not a sign of religion; it is a sign of subservience. It will not be welcome on the territory of the French republic" (BBC News, 2009). On September 14, 2010, the French senate—with Sarkozy's strong support—banned any veils covering the face, which included the burka.

In Switzerland, neoliberalism and xenophobia were evident in the politi-cal success of the conservative Swiss People's Party in the 2007 election. A political poster used by the Party showed three white sheep kicking a black sheep off a Swiss flag above the slogan, "For more security" (Charter, 2007). In the election that took place on Sunday, October 21, the People's Party gained the highest percent of votes in the parliamentary election of any party since shortly after World War I. Neoliberalism in Canada was exempli-fied in a call for social cohesion (Joshee, 2009). In Britain, multiculturalism was blamed for fracturing the nation after the London underground bombings in 2005 (Tomlinson, 2009). Writes Tomlinson,

> There were many suggestions that a once cohesive British society had been fractured by the presence of racial and ethnic groups and the arrival of newer economic migrants, refugees, and asylum seekers…A major political reaction was to focus on concepts of *community cohesion* and *integration* into an undefined "British" society, with little acknowledgement that the society had always been divided along lines of social class, wealth, gender, race, religion, and region. (p. 121) [italics added]

THE DEBATE BETWEEN THE ASSIMILATIONISTS AND MULTICULTURALISTS

Neoliberal and political conservatives claim that multiculturalism is detrimental to the nation-state and the civic community (Patterson, 1977; Schlesinger, 1991). Multiculturalists maintain that *civic equality, recognition,* (Gutmann, 2004) and *structural inclusion* into the nation-state are essential for citizens from diverse groups to acquire allegiance to the nation-state and to become effective participants in the civic community (Banks, 2007; Kymlicka, 2004).

I hope to make a scholarly contribution to the debate between the assimilationists and the multiculturalists in this chapter by providing evidence for the claim that the positions of both groups reflect values, ideologies, political positions, and human interests. Each position also implies a kind of knowledge that should be taught in the schools, colleges, and universities, and in public sites such as museums, theaters, films, and other visual media. I will describe a typology of the kinds of knowledge that exist in society and in educational institutions. This typology is designed to help practicing educators, researchers, and cultural workers to identify types of knowledge that reflect specific values, assumptions, perspectives, and ideological positions.

Educators and cultural workers should help students to understand all types of knowledge. Students should be involved in the debates about knowledge construction and conflicting interpretations, such as the extent to which Egypt and Phoenicia influenced Greek civilization (Bernal, 1987/1991). Students should also be taught how to construct their own interpretations of the past and present, as well as how to identify their own positions, interests, ideologies, and assumptions. Students should become critical thinkers who have the knowledge, attitudes, skills, and commitments needed to participate in democratic action to help their nation and the world close the gap between ideals and realities. Multicultural education is an education for functioning effectively in a pluralistic democratic society.

Helping students to develop the knowledge, skills, and attitudes needed to participate in reflective civic action is one of its major goals (Banks, 2007).

The philosophical position that underlies this chapter is within the transformative tradition in ethnic studies and multicultural education (Banks, 1996). This tradition links *knowledge, social commitment*, and *action* (Meier & Rudwick, 1986). A transformative, action-oriented education can best be implemented when students examine different types of knowledge, freely examine their perspectives and moral commitments, and experience democracy in schools (Dewey, 1938), and in public sites such as museums, theaters, and historical monuments (Loewen, 1999).

THE CHARACTERISTICS OF KNOWLEDGE

I define knowledge as the way an individual explains or interprets reality. I conceptualize knowledge broadly, and use it the way it is utilized in the sociology of knowledge literature to include ideas, values, and interpretations (Farganis, 1986). As postmodern theorists have pointed out, knowledge is socially constructed and reflects human interests, values, and action (Code, 1991; Foucault, 1972; Harding, 1991). Knowledge is also a product of human interactions (Nejadmehr, 2009). Writes Nejadmehr, "knowledge is always knowledge of contingent human conditions. Hence, the source of knowledge is changing cultural contexts" (p. 3). Although many complex factors influence the knowledge that is created by an individual or group— including the actuality of what occurred and the interactions that knowledge constructors have with other people—the knowledge that people create is heavily influenced by their interpretations of their experiences and their positions within particular social, economic, and political systems and structures of society.

In the Western empirical tradition, the ideal within each academic discipline is the formation of knowledge without the influence of the researcher's personal or cultural characteristics (Greer, 1969; Kaplan, 1964). However, as critical and postmodern theorists have pointed out, personal, cultural, and social factors influence the formulation of knowledge even when objective knowledge is the ideal within a discipline (Cherryholmes, 1988; Foucault, 1972; Habermas, 1971). Researchers are frequently unaware of how their personal experiences and positions within society influence the knowledge they produce. Most mainstream historians were unaware of how their regional and cultural biases influenced their interpretation of the Reconstruction period of U.S. history until W. E. B. DuBois (1935/1962) published a study that challenged the accepted and established interpretations of that historical period.

POSITIONALITY AND KNOWLEDGE CONSTRUCTION

Positionality is a significant concept which emerged out of feminist scholarship that describes how important aspects of identity such as gender, race, social class, age, religion, and sexual orientation influence the knowledge that scholars construct (Collins, 2000; Tetreault, 2007). Positionality reveals the importance of identifying the positions and frames of reference from which scholars and writers present their data, interpretations, and analyses (Anzaldúa, 1990). The need for researchers and scholars to identify their ideological positions and the normative assumptions in their work—an inherent part of feminist and ethnic studies scholarship—contrasts with the empirical paradigm that has dominated Western science (Code, 1991; Harding, 1991).

The assumption within the Western empirical paradigm is that the knowledge produced within it is neutral and objective and that its principles are universal. The effects of values, frames of references, and the normative positions of researchers and scholars are infrequently discussed within the traditional empirical paradigm that has dominated scholarship and teaching in colleges and universities in the West since the early twentieth century. However, scholars such as the Swedish economist Gunnar Myrdal (1944), and the American psychologist Kenneth B. Clark (1965)—prior to the feminist, ethnic studies, and postmodern movements—wrote about the need for scholars to recognize and state their normative positions and valuations and to become, in the apt words of Clark, "involved observers." Myrdal stated that valuations are not just attached to research but permeate it. He wrote, *"There is no device for excluding biases in social sciences than to face the valuations and to introduce them as explicitly stated, specific, and sufficiently concretized value premises"* (p. 1043) [emphasis in original].

A KNOWLEDGE TYPOLOGY

A description of the major types of knowledge can help educators and cultural workers to identify perspectives and content needed to make education multicultural and culturally responsive (Gay, 2000). Each of the types of knowledge described below reflects specific purposes, perspectives, experiences, goals, and human interests. Teaching students various types of knowledge can help them to better understand the perspectives of different racial, ethnic, and cultural groups as well as to develop their own versions and interpretations of issues and events. Different types of knowledge also help students to gain more comprehensive and accurate conceptions of reality. Multiple perspectives and different types of knowledge enable knowers to construct knowledge that is closer approximations to the actuality of what occurred than single perspectives. In an important and influential essay, Merton (1972) maintains that the perspectives of both "insiders" and "outsiders" are needed to enable social scientists to gain a comprehensive view of social reality.

I identify and describe five types of knowledge (see Figure 4.1):

1. *Personal/Cultural Knowledge*
2. *Popular Knowledge*
3. *Mainstream Academic Knowledge*
4. *Transformative Academic Knowledge*
5. *Pedagogical Knowledge*

This is an ideal-type typology in the Weberian sense. The German sociologist Max Weber pioneered the idea of using typologies to classify social phenomenon. His typology of three forms of authority—traditional, rational-legal, and charismatic—is an example (Henry, nd). The five categories of my knowledge typology, like the categories in Weber's typology, approximate but do not describe reality in its total complexity. The categories are useful conceptual tools for thinking about knowledge and planning multicultural teaching and learning. Although the categories can be conceptually distinguished, in reality they overlap and are interrelated in a dynamic way.

Since the 1960s, some of the findings and insights from transformative academic knowledge have been incorporated into mainstream academic knowledge and scholarship. Traditionally, students were taught in the U.S.

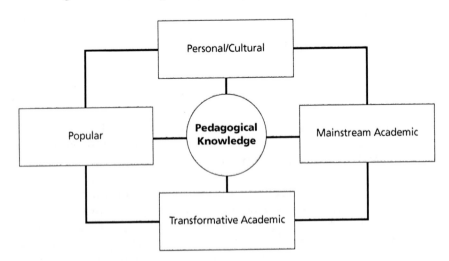

Figure 4.1 This figure illustrates how the five types of knowledge are interrelated. Copyright © 2011 by James A. Banks.

schools and universities that the land that became North America was a thinly populated wilderness when the Europeans arrived in the 16th century and that African Americans made few contributions to the development of American civilization (mainstream academic knowledge). Some of the findings from transformative academic knowledge that challenged these conceptions have influenced mainstream academic scholarship and have been incorporated into mainstream college, university, and school textbooks (Hoxie, nd; Thornton, 1987). Consequently, the relationship between the five categories of knowledge is dynamic and interactive rather than static.

THE TYPES OF KNOWLEDGE

Personal and Cultural Knowledge

The concepts, explanations, and interpretations that students derive from personal experiences in their homes, families, and community cultures constitute personal and cultural knowledge. The assumptions, perspectives, and insights that students derive from their experiences in their homes and community cultures are used as screens to view and interpret the knowledge and experiences they encounter in school and in other institutions and sites within the larger society, such as museums and the media.

Research and theory by Fordham and Ogbu (1986) indicate that low-income African American students often experience academic difficulties in school because of the ways that cultural knowledge within their community conflicts with pedagogical knowledge and with school norms and expectations. Fordham and Ogbu also state that the culture of many low-income African American students is oppositional to school culture. These students believe that if they master the knowledge taught in the schools they will violate fictive kinship norms and run the risk of "acting White." Fordham (1988, 1991) has suggested that African American students who become high academic achievers resolve the conflict caused by the interaction of their personal cultural knowledge with the knowledge and norms within the schools by becoming "raceless" or by "ad hocing a culture."

Personal and cultural knowledge is problematic when it conflicts with scientific ways of validating knowledge, is oppositional to the culture of the school, or challenges the main tenets and assumptions of mainstream academic knowledge. Much of the knowledge about out-groups that students learn from their home and community cultures consists of misconceptions, stereotypes, and inaccurate information (Aboud, 2009). Many students around the world are socialized within communities that are segregated along racial, ethnic, and social-class lines (Banks, 2009). These youths have few opportunities to learn firsthand about the cultures of people from different racial, ethnic, cultural, religious, and social-class groups.

The challenge for educators is to make effective instructional use of the personal and cultural knowledge of students while at the same time helping them to reach beyond their cultural boundaries (Moll & González, 2004; Lee, 2007). Educational institutions should recognize, validate, and make effective use of student personal and cultural knowledge. However, an important goal of education is to free students from their cultural and ethnic boundaries and enable them to cross cultural borders freely (Banks, 2007).

In the past, the school and other educational institutions have paid little attention to the personal and cultural knowledge of students and have taught them mainly popular and mainstream knowledge. It is important for teachers and cultural workers to be aware of the personal and cultural knowledge of students when designing educational experiences for students from diverse groups. Educators can use student personal cultural knowledge to motivate them and as a foundation and scaffold for teaching other types of knowledge (Ladson-Billings, 1994).

POPULAR KNOWLEDGE

Popular knowledge consists of the facts, interpretations, and beliefs that are institutionalized within television, movies, videos, DVDs, CDs, and other forms of mass media. Many of the tenets of popular knowledge are conveyed in subtle rather than explicit ways (Cortés, 2000). These statements are examples of significant themes in U.S. popular knowledge:

1. The United States is a powerful nation with unlimited opportunities for individuals who are willing to take advantage of them.
2. To succeed in the United States, an individual only has to work hard. You can realize your dreams in the United States if you are willing to work hard and pull yourself up by the bootstrap.
3. As a land of opportunity for all, the United States is a highly cohesive nation, whose ideals of equality and freedom are shared by all.

Most of the major tenets of American popular culture are widely shared and are deeply entrenched in U.S. society. However, they are rarely explicitly articulated. Rather, they are presented in the media, in museums (Sherman, 2008), historical sites (Loewen, 1999), and in other sources in the forms of stories, anecdotes, news stories, and interpretations of current events (Cortés, 2000). In his engaging and informative book, *Lies Across America: What Our Historic Sites Get Wrong*, Loewen describes how historical sites in the United States perpetuate and reinforce popular myths about American heroes, events, and exceptionalism.

Commercial entertainment films both reflect and perpetuate popular knowledge (Shohat & Stam, 1994). While preparing to write this chapter I viewed *How the West Was Won*, a popular and influential film that was directed by John Ford and released by MGM in 1962. I selected this film for review because the settlement of the West is a major theme in American culture and society about which there are many popular images, beliefs, myths, and misconceptions. In viewing the film, I was particularly interested in the images it depicted about the settlement of the West, about the people who were already in the West, and about people who went west looking for new opportunities.

Ford uses the Prescotts, a White family from Missouri bound for California, to tell his story. The film tells the story of three generations of the Prescott family. It focuses on the family's struggle to settle in the West. Indians, African Americans, and Mexicans are largely invisible in the film. Indians appear in the story when they attack the Prescott family during their long and perilous journey. The Mexicans appearing in the film are bandits who rob a train and are killed. The several African Americans in the film are in the background silently rowing a boat. At various points in the film, Indians are referred to as *hostile Indians* and as *squaws*.

How the West Was Won is a masterpiece in American popular culture. It not only depicts some of the major themes in American culture about the winning of the West; it reinforces and perpetuates dominant societal attitudes, folk beliefs, and myths about ethnic groups and gives credence to the notion that the West was won by liberty-loving, hard-working people who pursued freedom for all. The film narrator states near its end, "[The movement West] produced a people free to dream, free to act, and free to mold their own destiny."

MAINSTREAM ACADEMIC KNOWLEDGE

Mainstream academic knowledge consists of the concepts, paradigms, theories, and explanations that constitute traditional and established knowledge in the behavioral and social sciences. An important tenet within the mainstream academic paradigm is that there is a set of objective truths that can be verified through rigorous and objective research procedures that are uninfluenced by human interests, values, and perspectives (Greer, 1969; Kaplan, 1964). This empirical knowledge constitutes a body of objective truths that should make up the core of the school and university curriculum. Much of this objective knowledge originated in the West but is considered universal in nature and application.

Mainstream academic knowledge is the knowledge that multicultural critics such as Ravitch and Finn (1987), Hirsch (1987), and Bloom (1987) claim is threatened by the addition of content about women and ethnic groups of color to the school, college, and university curriculum. This knowledge reflects the established, Western-oriented canon that has historically dominated university research and teaching in Western nations. Mainstream academic knowledge consists of the theories and interpretations that are internalized and accepted by most university researchers, academic societies, and organizations such as the American Historical Association, the American Sociological Association, the American Psychological Association, and the National Academy of Sciences.

An increasing number of university scholars are critical theorists and postmodernists who question the empirical paradigm that dominates Western science (Cherryholmes, 1988; Giroux, 1983; Rosenau, 1992). Many of these individuals are members of national academic organizations such as the American Historical Association and the American Sociological Association. In most of these professional organizations, the postmodern scholars—made up of significant numbers of scholars of color and feminists—have formed caucuses and interest groups within the mainstream professional organizations.

I am not claiming that there is a uniformity of belief among mainstream academic scholars, but rather that there are dominant canons, paradigms, and theories that are accepted by the community of mainstream academic scholars and researchers. These established canons and paradigms are occasionally challenged within the mainstream academic community itself. However, they receive their most serious challenges from academics outside the mainstream, such as scholars within the transformative academic community described later (Collins, 2000; Takaki, 1993; hooks, 1994; Okihiro, 1994).

Mainstream academic knowledge, like the other forms of knowledge discussed in this chapter, is not static, but is *dynamic, complex, and changing.* Challenges to the dominant canons and paradigms within mainstream academic knowledge come from both within and without. These challenges lead to changes, reinterpretations, debates, disagreements, paradigm shifts, and to new theories and interpretations. Kuhn (1970) states that a scientific revolution takes place when a new paradigm emerges and replaces an existing one. What is more typical in education and the social sciences is that competing paradigms coexist, although particular ones are more influential during certain times or periods.

We can examine the treatment of slavery within the mainstream academic community over time, or the treatment of the American Indian, to identify ways that mainstream academic knowledge has changed in important ways since the late nineteenth and early twentieth centuries in the United

States. Ulrich B. Phillips' highly influential book, *American Negro Slavery*, published in 1918, dominated the way Black slavery was interpreted until his views were challenged by researchers in the 1950s (Stampp, 1956). Phillips was a respected authority on the antebellum South and on slavery. His book, which became a historical classic, is essentially an apology for Southern slaveholders (Smith & Inscoe, 1993). A new paradigm about slavery was developed in the 1970s that drew heavily upon the slaves' view of their own experiences (Blassingame, 1972; Gutman, 1976).

During the late nineteenth and early twentieth centuries, the American Indian was portrayed in mainstream academic knowledge as either a noble or a hostile savage (Hoxie, 1988). Other notions that became institutionalized within mainstream academic knowledge include the idea that Columbus discovered America and that America was a thinly populated frontier when the Europeans arrived in the late fifteenth century. In his influential paper, "The Significance of the Frontier in American History," Frederick Jackson Turner (1894/1989) argued that the frontier, which he regarded as a wilderness, was the main source of American democracy. Although Turner's thesis is now criticized by revisionist historians, his essay established a conception of the West that has been highly influential in American mainstream scholarship, in the popular culture, and in schoolbooks. The conception of the West constructed by Turner is still influential in the school curriculum and in textbooks (Sleeter & Grant, 1991).

These ideas also became institutionalized within mainstream academic knowledge: The slaves were happy and contented; most of the important ideas that became a part of American civilization came from Western Europe; and the history of the United States has been one of constantly expanding progress and increasing democracy. African slaves were needed to transform the United States from an empty wildness into an industrial democratic civilization. The American Indians had to be Christianized and removed to reservations in order for the United States to become an industrialized nation.

TRANSFORMATIVE ACADEMIC KNOWLEDGE

Transformative academic knowledge consists of concepts, paradigms, themes, and explanations that challenge mainstream academic knowledge and that expand the historical and literary canon. Transformative academic knowledge challenges some of the key assumptions that mainstream scholars make about the nature of knowledge. Transformative and mainstream academic knowledge are based on different epistemological assumptions about the nature of knowledge, about the influence of human interests and values on knowledge construction, and about the purpose of knowledge.

An important tenet of mainstream academic knowledge is that it is neutral, objective, and is uninfluenced by human interests and values. Transformative academic knowledge reflects postmodern assumptions and goals about the nature and goals of knowledge (Foucault, 1972; Rorty, 1989; Rosenau, 1992). Transformative academic scholars assume that knowledge is not neutral but is influenced by human interests, that all knowledge reflects the power and social relationships within society, and that an important purpose of knowledge construction is to help people improve society (Code, 1991; Harding, 1991; King & Mitchell, 1990). Knowledge and its construction are linked to action and the improvement of society to make it more just and humane.

These statements reflect some of the significant ideas and concepts in transformative academic knowledge in the United States: Columbus did not discover America. The Indians had been living in the Americas for about 40,000 years when the Europeans arrived. Concepts such as "The European Discovery of America" and "The Westward Movement" need to be reconceptualized and viewed from the perspectives of different cultural and ethnic groups. The Lakota Sioux's homeland was not the West to them; it was the center of the universe. It was not West for the Alaskans; it was South. It was East for the Japanese and North for the people who lived in Mexico. The history of the United States has not been one of continuous progress toward democratic ideals (Appleby, 1992). Rather, the nation's history has been characterized by a cyclic quest for democracy and by conflict, struggle, violence, and exclusion (Acuña, 1988; Zinn, 1980). A major challenge for the United States is how to make its democratic ideals a reality for all of its citizens.

PEDAGOGICAL KNOWLEDGE

Pedagogical knowledge consists of the facts, concepts, and generalizations presented in textbooks, teachers' guides, and other forms of media designed for instruction. Pedagogical knowledge also consists of the mediation and interpretation of the information in instructional materials and resources. The textbook is the main source of pedagogical knowledge in schools the United States (Apple & Christian-Smith, 1991). Studies of textbooks indicate that these are some of the major themes in pedagogical knowledge in the United States (Sleeter & Grant, 1991; Loewen, 2010):

1. America's founding fathers, such as Washington and Jefferson, were highly moral, liberty-loving men who championed equality and justice for all Americans.
2. The United States is a nation with justice, liberty, and freedom for all.

3. Social class divisions are not significant issues in the United States.
4. There is no significant gender, class, or racial divisions within U.S. society.
5. Ethnic groups of color and Whites interact harmoniously in the United States.

TRANSFORMATIVE AND MAINSTREAM CITIZENSHIP EDUCATION

Transformative citizenship education—which is rooted in transformative academic knowledge—enables students to acquire the knowledge, skills, and values needed to challenge inequality within their communities, nation, and the world, and to take actions to create just and democratic multicultural communities and societies (Banks, 2007). Transformative citizenship education helps students to develop decision-making and social action skills that are needed to identify problems in society, acquire knowledge related to them, identify and clarify their values, and to take thoughtful individual and/or effective collective action (Banks, Banks, & Clegg, 1999).

Students must experience just and democratic schools, classrooms, and public sites in order to internalize democratic values. Consequently, the school and public sites such as museums and historical monuments must be reconstructed in order to implement transformative citizenship education. Existing power relationships are challenged and are not reproduced in transformative democratic classrooms and schools. Transformative citizenship education, which takes place in democratic schools, fosters equality and recognition for students from diverse groups, and helps students acquire the knowledge and skills needed to take action to make their communities, the nation, and the world just places in which to live.

Mainstream citizenship education, which is grounded in mainstream knowledge and assumptions, reinforces the status quo and the dominant power relationships in society. It does not challenge or disrupt the class, racial, and gender discrimination within educational institutions or society. The emphasis in mainstream citizenship education is on memorizing facts about constitutions and other legal documents, learning about various branches of government, and developing loyalty to the nation-state. Critical thinking skills, decision-making, and action are not important components of mainstream citizenship education. It is practiced in most social studies classrooms in many nations, including the United States, Canada, and the United Kingdom.

TRANSFORMATIVE CITIZENSHIP EDUCATION
AND EDUCATIONAL REFORM

Citizenship education must be transformed in order to help students to acquire the knowledge, values, and skills needed to become cosmopolitan citizens who have a commitment to act to make their communities, nation, and the world more just and humane (Banks, 2007). A holistic paradigm, which conceptualizes the educational institution as an interrelated whole, is needed to implement transformative citizenship education (see Figure 4.2). Conceptualizing the educational institution as a social system can help educators to develop effective reform strategies that will enable students to acquire the knowledge, attitudes, and values needed to participate in reflective decision-making and citizen action (Newmann, 1975). Both research and theory indicate that educators can successfully intervene to help students to increase their academic achievement (Lee, 2007), and to develop democratic attitudes and values (Banks & Banks, 2004; Stephan & Vogt, 2004).

Conceptualizing the educational institution as a social system means that educators should formulate and initiate a change strategy that reforms the total institutional environment in order to implement transformative citizenship education that promotes social justice and human rights. Reforming

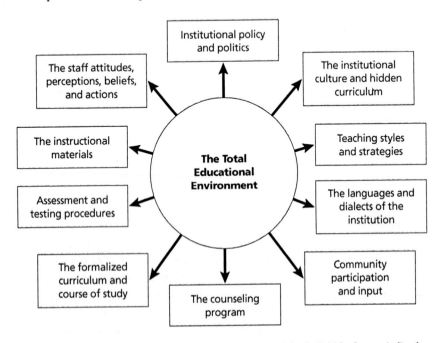

Figure 4.2   The Total Educational Environment. Copyright © 2012 by James A. Banks.

any one variable, such as curriculum materials and the formal curriculum, is necessary but not sufficient. Multicultural and sensitive teaching materials are ineffective in the hands of instructors who have negative attitudes and low expectations for students from diverse ethnic, cultural, linguistic, and religious groups. Such instructors are likely to use multicultural materials rarely or to use them in a detrimental way when they do. Thus, helping instructors and other members of the institution to develop democratic attitudes and values is essential when implementing transformative citizenship education (Green, 2005).

TRANSFORMATIVE DEMOCRATIC CITIZENS

Schools of tomorrow should implement transformative citizenship education. The goal of transformative citizenship education is to socialize students who will become socially committed, active, and transformative citizens. The characteristics of transformative citizens in a multicultural democratic society are summarized in Figure 4.3. These citizens have democratic attitudes

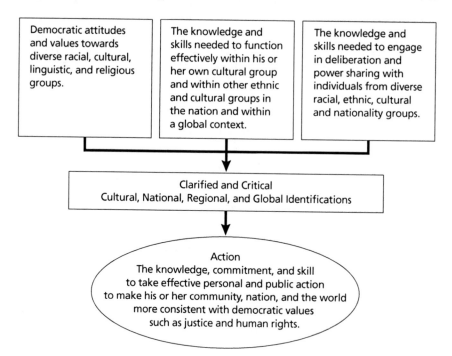

Figure 4.3 Characteristics of the effective citizen in a multicultural democratic society. Copyright © 2011 by James A. Banks.

and values toward diverse groups, and the knowledge and skills needed to function within their own cultural group as well as within other ethnic and cultural groups in the nation, region, and global community. They also have the knowledge and skills needed to engage in deliberation and power sharing with individuals from other racial, ethnic, cultural, linguistic, and religious groups. The transformative citizen also has clarified and reflective cultural, national, regional, and global identifications as well as the knowledge, commitment, and skills needed to act to promote social justice and human rights within their local communities, nation, region, and the global community. It is imperative that schools of tomorrow prepare transformative citizens who have the knowledge, commitment, and skills needed to make our nation and world more just and humane.

ACKNOWLEDGEMENT

This chapter is a revised version of a paper presented as the keynote address at the conference Interkulturell Pedagogik, September 23, 2009, held at the Göteborg Convention Centre, Gothenburg, Sweden. Parts of it are adapted from James A. Banks, The canon debate, knowledge construction, and multicultural education. *Educational Researcher, 22*(5), 4–14, 1993; and James A. Banks, The lives and values of researchers: Implications for educating citizens in a multicultural society. *Educational Researcher, 27*(7), 4–17, 1998. Used with permission of the American Educational Research Association.

REFERENCES

Aboud, F. (2009). Modifying children's racial attitudes. In J. A. Banks (Ed.), *The Routledge international companion to multicultural education* (pp. 199–209). New York & London: Routledge.

Acuña, R. (1988). *Occupied America: A history of Chicanos* (3rd ed.). New York: Harper & Row.

Appiah, K. A. (2006). *Cosmopolitanism: Ethics in a world of strangers.* New York: Norton.

Apple, M. W., & Christian-Smith, L. K. (Eds.). (1991). *The politics of the textbook.* New York: Routledge.

Appleby, J. (1992). Recovering America's historic diversity: Beyond exceptionalism. *The Journal of American History, 79*(2), 419–431.

d'Appollonia, A. C., & Reich, S. (Eds.). (2008). *Immigration, integration, and security: America and Europe in contemporary perspective.* Pittsburg, PA: University of Pittsburgh Press.

Anzaldúa, G. (1990). Haciendo caras, una entrada: An introduction. In G. Anzaldúa (Ed.), *Making face, making soul: Haciendo caras* (pp. xv–xvii). San Francisco: Aunt Lute Foundation Books.

Baldwin, J. (1953/1985). Stranger in the village. In J. Baldwin, *The price of the ticket: Collected nonfiction 1948–1985* (pp. 79–90). New York: St. Martin's.

Banks, J. A. (Ed.). (1996). *Multicultural education, transformative knowledge, and action: Historical and contemporary perspectives.* New York: Teachers College Press.

Banks, J. A. (1998). The lives and values of researchers: Implications for educating citizens in a multicultural society. *Educational Researcher, 27*(7), 4–17.

Banks, J. A. (2007). *Educating citizens in a multicultural society* (2nd ed.). New York: Teachers College Press.

Banks, J. A. (Ed.). (2009). *The Routledge international companion to multicultural education.* New York & London: Routledge.

Banks, J. A., & Banks. C. A. M. (Eds.). (2004). *Handbook of research on multicultural education* (2nd ed.). San Francisco: Jossey-Bass.

Banks, J. A., Banks, C. A. M., & Clegg, A. A., Jr. (1999). *Teaching strategies for the social studies: Decision-making and citizen action.* New York: Longman.

BBC News (2009, June 22). *Sarkozy speaks out against burka.* Retrieved July 4, 2009 from http://news.bbc.co.uk/2/hi/europe/8112821.stm

Bernal, M. (1987/1991). *Black Athena: The Afroasiatic roots of classical civilization* (Vols. 1/2). London: Free Association Books.

Blassingame, J. W. (1972). *The slave community: Plantation life in the Antebellum South.* New York: Oxford University Press.

Bloom, A. (1987). *The closing of the American mind.* New York: Simon & Schuster.

Bowen, J. R. (2007). *Why the French don't like headscarves: Islam, the state, and the public space.* Princeton, NJ: Princeton University Press.

Charter, D. (2007, October 10). 'Black sheep' cartoon ignites bitter row on racism before Swiss election. *Timesonline.* Retrieved April 26, 2009 from http://www.timesonline.co.uk/tol/news/world/europe/article2625385.ece

Cherryholmes, C. H. (1988). *Power and criticism: Postructural investigations in education.* New York: Teachers College Press.

Clark, K. B. (1965). *Dark ghetto: Dilemmas of social power.* New York: Harper & Row.

Code, L. (1991). *What can she know? Feminist theory and the construction of knowledge.* Ithaca, NY: Cornell University Press.

Collins, P. H. (2000). *Black feminist thought: Knowledge, consciousness, and the politics of empowerment* (2nd ed.). New York: Routledge.

Cortés, C. E. (2000). *The children are watching: How the media teach about diversity.* New York: Teachers College Press.

Dewey, J. (1938). *Experience and education.* New York: Macmillan.

Du Bois, W. E. B. (1935/1962). *Black reconstruction in America 1860–1880: An essay toward a history of the part which Black folk played in the attempt to reconstruct democracy in America, 1860–1880.* New York: Atheneum.

Farganis, S. (1986). *The social construction of the feminine character.* Totowa, NJ: Russell & Russell.

Fordham, S. (1988). Racelessness as a factor in Black students' school success: Pragmatic strategy or Pyrrhic victory? *Harvard Educational Review, 58,* 54–84.

Fordham, S. (1991). Racelessness in private schools: Should we deconstruct the racial and cultural identity of African-American adolescents? *Teachers College Record, 92,* 470–484.

Fordham, S., & Ogbu, J. (1986). Black students' school success: Coping with the burden of 'acting White.' *The Urban Review, 18,* 176–206.

Foucault, M. (1972). *The archaeology of knowledge and the discourse on language.* New York: Pantheon.

Gay, G. (2000). *Culturally responsive teaching: Theory, research, and practice.* New York: Teachers College Press.

Giroux, H. A. (1983). *Theory and resistance in education.* Boston: Bergin & Garvey.

Gutmann, A. (2004). Unity and diversity in democratic multicultural education: Creative and destructive tensions. In J. A. Banks (Ed.), *Diversity and citizenship education: Global perspectives* (pp. 71–96). San Francisco: Jossey-Bass.

Gutman, H. G. (1976). *The Black family in slavery and freedom 1750–1925.* New York: Vintage.

Green, R. L. (2005). *Expectations: How teacher expectations can increase student achievement and assist in closing the achievement gap.* Columbus, OH: McGraw-Hill SRA.

Greer, S. (1969). *The logic of social inquiry.* Chicago: Aldine.

Habermas, J. (1971). *Knowledge and human interests.* Boston: Beacon.

Harding, S. (1991). *Whose science? Whose knowledge? Thinking from women's lives.* Ithaca, NY: Cornell University Press.

Henry, K. (nd). *Max Weber's typology of forms of authority—traditional, rational-legal, and charismatic.* Retrieved August 16, 2009 from http://ezinearticles.com/?Max-Webers-Typology-of-Forms-of-Authority-Traditional,-Rational-Legal,-and-Charismatic&id=507723\

Herrnstein, R. J., & Murray, C. (1994). *The bell curve: Intelligence and class structure in American life.* New York: The Free Press.

Hirsch, E. D., Jr. (1987). *Cultural literacy: What every American needs to know.* Boston: Houghton Mifflin.

hooks, b. (1994). *Teaching to transgress: Education as the practice of freedom.* New York: Routledge.

Hoxie, F. E. (nd). *The Indians versus the textbooks: Is there any way out?* Chicago: The Newberry Library, Center for the History of the American Indian.

Hoxie, F. E. (Ed.). (1988). *Indians in American history.* Arlington Heights, IL: Harlan Davidson.

Joshee, R. (2009). Multicultural education policy in Canada: Competing ideologies, interconnected discourses. In J. A. Banks (Ed.), *The Routledge international companion to multicultural education* (pp. 96–108). New York & London: Routledge.

Kaplan, A. (1964*). The conduct of inquiry: Methodology for behavioral science.* San Francisco: Chandler.

King, J. L. (1995). Culture-centered knowledge: Black studies, curriculum transformation, and social action. In J. A. Banks & C. A. M. Banks (Eds.), *Handbook of research on multicultural education* (pp. 265–290). New York: Macmillan.

King, J. E., & Mitchell, C. A. (1990). *Black mothers to sons: Juxtaposing African-American literature with social practice.* New York: Lang.

Kuhn, T. S. (1970). *The structure of scientific revolutions* (2nd ed.). Chicago: University of Chicago Press.

Kymlicka, W. (2004). Foreword. In J. A. Banks (Ed.), *Diversity and citizenship education: Global perspectives* (pp. xiii–xviii). San Francisco: Jossey-Bass.

Ladner, J. A. (Ed.). (1973). *The death of White sociology.* New York: Vintage.

Lee, C. D. (2007). *Culture, literacy, and learning: Taking bloom in the midst of the whirlwind.* New York: Teachers College Press.

Ladson-Billings, G. (1994). *The dreamkeepers: Successful teachers of African-American children.* San Francisco: Jossey-Bass.

Loewen, J. W. (2010). *Teaching what really happened: How to avoid the tyranny of textbooks and get students really excited about doing history.* New York: Teachers College Press.

Loewen, J. W. (1999). *Lies across America: What our historic sites get wrong.* New York: The New Press.

Meier, A., & Rudwick, E. (1986). *Black history and the historical profession 1915–1980.* Urbana, IL: University of Illinois Press.

Merton, R. K. (1972). Insiders and outsiders: A chapter in the sociology of knowledge. *The American Journal of Sociology, 78,* 9–47.

Moll, L. C., & Gonzalez, N. (2004). Engaging life: A funds-of-knowledge approach to multicultural education. In J. A. Banks & C. A. M. Banks (Eds.), *Handbook of research on multicultural education* (2nd ed., pp. 699–715). San Francisco: Jossey-Bass.

Myrdal, G. (with the assistance of R. Sterner & A. Rose). (1944). *An American dilemma: The Negro problem in modern democracy.* New York: Harper.

Nejadmehr, R. (2009). *Education, science and truth.* New York & London: Routledge.

Newmann, F. M. (1975). *Education for citizen action: Challenge for secondary curriculum.* Berkeley, CA: McCutchan.

Okihiro, G. Y. (1994). *Margins and mainstreams: Asians in American history and culture.* Seattle: University of Washington Press.

Painter, N. I. (2006). *Creating Black Americans: African-American history and its meanings: 1619 to the present.* New York: Oxford University Press.

Patterson, O. (1977). *Ethnic chauvinism: The reactionary impulse.* New York: Stein and Day.

Phillips, U. B. (1918/1966). *American Negro slavery.* Baton Rouge: Louisiana State University Press.

Ravitch, D., & Finn, C. E., Jr. (1987). *What do our 17-year-olds know? A report on the first national assessment of history and literature.* New York: Harper & Row.

Rorty, R. (1989). *Contingency, irony, and solidarity.* New York: Cambridge University Press.

Rosenau, P. M. (1992). *Post-modernism and the social sciences.* Princeton, NJ: Princeton University Press.

Schlesinger, A., Jr. (1991). *The disuniting of America: Reflections on a multicultural society.* Knoxville, TN: Whittle Direct Books.

Scott, J. W. (2007). *Politics of the veil.* Princeton, NJ: Princeton University Press.

Sherman, D. J. (Ed.). (2008). *Museums and difference.* Bloomington, IN: Indiana University Press.

Shohat, E., & Stam, R. (1994). *Unthinking Eurocentrism: Multiculturalism and the media.* London & New York: Routledge.

Sleeter, C. E., & Grant. C. A. (1991). Race, class, gender and disability in current textbooks. In M. W. Apple & L. K. Christian-Smith (Eds.). *The politics of textbooks* (pp. 78–110). New York: Routledge.

Smith, J. D., & Inscoe, J. C. (Eds.). (1993). *Ulrich Bonnell Phillips: A Southern historian and his critics.* Athens: The University of Georgia Press.

Stampp, K. M. (1956). *The peculiar institution: Slavery in the ante-bellum South.* New York: Vintage.

Stephan, W. G., & Vogt, W. P. (Eds.). (2004). *Education programs for improving intergroup relations: Theory, research, and practice.* New York: Teachers College Press.

Takaki, R. (1993). *A different mirror: A history of multicultural America.* Boston: Little, Brown.

Tetreault, M. K. T. (2007). Classrooms for diversity: Rethinking curriculum and pedagogy. In J. A. Banks & C. A. M. Banks (Eds.), *Multicultural education: Issues and perspectives* (6th ed., pp. 171–193). Hoboken, NJ: Wiley.

Thornton, R. (1987). *American Indian holocaust and survival: A population history since 1492.* Norman: University of Oklahoma Press.

Tomlinson, S. (2009). Multicultural education in the United Kingdom. In J. A. Banks (Ed.), *The Routledge international companion to multicultural education* (pp. 121–133). New York & London: Routledge.

Turner, F. J. (1894/1989). The significance of the frontier in American history. In C. A. Milner II (Ed.), *Major problems in the history of the American West* (pp. 2–21). Lexington, MA: Heath.

Zinn, H. (1980). *A people's history of the United States.* New York: Harper & Row.

CHAPTER 5

WORRYING ABOUT DIVERSITY OF A DIFFERENT KIND

David C. Berliner
Arizona State University

In recent decades when people talk about diversity, or lately superdiversity, they are referring to the many new legal and illegal immigrants to our cities, countries, and schools. These people of different colors, religions, culture, customs, food preferences, clothing, and most importantly different childrearing practices, are a challenge to the schools for two reasons. One is that the public schools of the majority of the developed world are not very adept at accommodating such differences, and the other is that many of the immigrants are poor and poorly educated. The movement of workers seeking jobs across borders is not likely to stop soon, and the schools of all the developed nations will struggle to find ways to make the children of immigrants into good citizens and good workers.

But there are at least four other kinds of diversity that need to be attended to in the schools of the future, namely, diversity in curriculum, diversity in conceptions of talent, diversity in assessment, and diversity in instruction.

Schooling for Tomorrow's America, pages 65–72
Copyright © 2014 by Information Age Publishing

I will describe what I see as the present trends in these areas, all of which lead to my worry about the future of schooling in the United States.

DIVERSITY IN CURRICULUM

It is now clear that in test-oriented cultures such as the United States and England, for those who are poor, the curriculum offered is increasingly standardized and has become much narrower. The new national standards in the United States, adopted by almost all states, will ensure through the national tests that accompany the standards, that we will know with reasonable certainty what all our nations' children are learning every month and year. This pleases most people. Not recognized, however, is that such uniformity in curriculum and assessment promotes homogeneity of outcomes. In test-oriented cultures, the curriculum delivered in classrooms is not what is in the state curriculum guides—it is that which will produce higher scores on the standardized tests used to judge teachers and schools. High-stakes testing invariably results in a narrowing of the curriculum delivered to our youth, and that curriculum is close to whatever is assessed on the tests.

Our nation's new tests will be predominantly in reading and mathematics, as was true of testing under the No Child Left Behind (NCLB) act. We anticipate, therefore, an increase in the time spent teaching those two subjects and a continued diminution in the time allocated for teaching other subjects. Research has demonstrated that this is what happens in test-oriented cultures (Berliner, 2011).

Under NCLB time for teaching social studies, government, and history has been substantially reduced in American schools. This occurs despite the cry from almost all Americans that the schools must fulfill their responsibility as institutions for the promotion and maintenance of our democracy. Instructional time for teaching science has been reduced because, under NCLB, the scores on science tests are not counted when determining school or district success. As a rule, instructional time is taken from untested subject matter areas and instructional time or time spent in test preparation is added to those areas that are to be covered on the tests. Time for teaching physical education has gone down, despite the fact that our youth are more sedentary, are frequently overweight, and Type 2 diabetes is becoming more common. Recess time and lunch time have been reduced, as well. Art and music, nationally, are down an average of at least an hour a week. This is particularly troublesome because our nation has never spent a lot of time in these subjects and yet their worth seems inestimable to many, including me. The arts can be justified on no other basis than it is proper for our society to be well-versed in and appreciative of the visual arts, music, dance, and theater. But, if need be, the arts can also be justified because they provide alternative ways of representing our worlds; by doing that, the arts have enhanced scientific and technological innovation, thereby helping the American economy. Arts for our schools, therefore, are not a frill. In every known culture the arts are a manifestation of human creativity. Therefore, attempts to limit instruction in the arts, particularly in the schools that serve the poor, are to limit human potential, and that is a very unhappy thought for the education community.

A way to think about the costs to society of a narrow, rather than a rich and diverse curriculum, is to hypothesize about the nature of the future. I see a future that is best characterized as Volatile, Uncertain, Complex, and Ambiguous, a VUCA world (Johanson, 2007). If, indeed, a VUCA world seems likely, I would want for my society the widest possible breadth of talent so that at least some of the talents that exist in society would be appropriate to whatever the world brings our way. I see evolution as a metaphor. In evolution, if characteristics of the niche that one inhabits change, only organisms that are adaptive will find the means to survive. In a VUCA world the social and occupational niches we inhabit will be under pressure. In times of rapid social change, therefore, variations in talents, like variations in genes, are needed. Identical skills in society, like identical genes in organisms, might not have survival value. So national standards for the design of curriculum, with states adopting highly similar tests, and the accompanying narrowing of the curriculum to meet the standards and increase tests scores, may be dangerous.

DIVERSITY IN CONCEPTIONS OF TALENT

Under a narrower curriculum with tests that are highly consequential for schools, teachers, and students, we end up valuing as "smart," talented, gifted, or successful, those students who produce the highest scores on the indicators we use to judge our schools, teachers, and students. Thus, reading skill and mathematics proficiency come to define what it means to be "smart" in school.

But the ability for students to excel in other areas, particularly those that are of inherent interest to them, seems almost unlimited. As examples of this we can think of our students' commitment to their hobbies, such as building robots, studying dinosaurs, learning about our civil war, collecting butterflies, and acquiring strategic and psychomotor skills in video games. But with high-stakes testing, students are not allocated school time to follow their interests unless those interests are aligned to the English language arts and the mathematics curriculum. Schools are not designed to value the skills the students have developed on their own. And, schools find ways to inform their students, in not very subtle ways, that the high level skills they have developed on their own do not demonstrate they are talented persons.

Our students also learn at an early age that the youngster who can fix any car or any computer is not very talented unless they also score high on the tests. They learn that the student who is terrific at organizing the cookie drive, the child that gives a great performance in the school play, or the child who does remarkable pencil sketches, are not really gifted unless they also get high scores on the tests. Sadly, so many of the skills that children have acquired on their own, or can demonstrate in school, are not valued unless accompanied by high scores in literacy and numeracy tests.

One curriculum size is now supposed to fit all our students. And the tests associated with that curriculum will naturally determine who is, and who is not, a successful student. Instead, I would argue we need more diversity in our conceptions of who is "smart," talented, gifted, and successful. Of course, we should not abandon the goal of high levels of literacy and numeracy for all of our nation's students. That is not what I am advocating. But simultaneously, we must also not abandon our commitment to the worth of all our youthful citizens. Innumerable adult Americans of substance in their personal lives and successful in their employment were not considered talented in the language arts and mathematics curricula during their youth. Their school experiences should not teach them that they are of lesser worth than others.

DIVERSITY IN ASSESSMENT

One of the major problems associated with high-stakes testing is the cost. Those who promulgate such assessments have to worry about the money required for the design, field test, psychometric analysis, administration, scoring, and feedback of the test results, as well as the reliability of any test that is consequential for those who take or are affected by the test results. Those costs go up as the number of constructed response items and short essays on a test increase.

Typically, more time is needed to complete constructed response items than multiple-choice items. And, typically, the larger the number of items on a test the more reliable it will be. So if you have a limited amount of time available for testing, then the more constructed response items that are on the test, the fewer the total number of test items on the test, and, therefore, the lower the reliability of the test. Furthermore, compared to multiple-choice items that can be scored rapidly and inexpensively by a machine, the constructed response items usually require slow, expensive and less reliable human judges. This, too, argues against their use.

Other ways of assessing students, such as with portfolios, group projects, oral presentations. and book reports are all harder to standardize, difficult to do on a mass scale, usually less reliable, and require the investment of considerable amounts of time and energy from teachers. So, despite the best intentions at the start of a testing program, by the end of such programs you find a very heavy reliance on multiple-choice items, or heavily constrained constructed response items, and these kinds of items all have one major troubling property.

Multiple-choice items almost always rely more heavily on memory than on reasoning, critical thinking, problem-solving, integration of ideas, and creative responses to problems' posed. But memory is now also a characteristic of iPhones and hard drives, readily available to us but not requiring any storage space in our brains. Throughout history excellent memory has long been a characteristic of the most educated: our storytellers, priests, scientists, engineers, masons, and cooks. But now weak and ordinary memories need no longer be a barrier for a candidate for these and many other jobs. On the other hand, modern businesses say they want knowledge workers: employees that can work in and with diverse groups; think critically, and who can both sense and solve problems. Over reliance on multiple-choice tests interferes with the attainment of these modern goals. Diversity in assessment strategies is needed to be sure that other cognitive processes besides memory have a chance to be displayed in our schools. Learning to think requires an apprenticeship in thinking.

DIVERSITY IN INSTRUCTION

Almost all educators agree that there can be too heavy a reliance on workbooks and computer drills, often done as seat work and often done as a part of test preparation in high-stakes testing cultures. But most educators also agree that there is definitely a place for these kinds of activities. After all, thinking requires knowledge of a domain in which some of that domain's facts and processes can be taught efficaciously through drill and practice, seatwork, and assessment with multiple-choice tests. But I am asking that we think about instruction differently. Each semester I would like to have teachers and students instruct their classes in something in which they are expert. This, then, becomes a curriculum, as well as an instructional issue. Following Kieran Egan's (2010) innovative proposals I would say it is the right of every student to have a subject assigned to them early in their school experience in which, under the guidance of teachers and others in a community, they would learn something in depth. The student, from their earliest experiences in school, would become expert in some area. The assigned subjects that they study, for a minimum of a number of years, could be airplanes, mollusks, the civil war, baboons, lizards, bugs, digital photography, flowering plants, or whatever was broadly educational, just as long as students became experts, and were allotted sufficient time to present their growing knowledge of the domain they study to their classmates and the broader school community, at least once per year. That diversifies both curriculum and instruction. It gives children the opportunity to learn the skills and put in the time needed to become expert at something, and by doing so, lets them experience the intellectual power that is achieved when one has expertise in some area. In addition, it provides them with a chance to teach others in the area about which they have commanding knowledge.

I would add to Egan's proposal, that it is also the right of every teacher, in spring and fall, to teach for up to one week anything they wanted, as long as it was a broadly educational subject that they loved and in which they had expertise. Students have a right to experience passionate teaching and expertise at work.

A literature teacher who loves *Moby Dick* and understands the context for nineteenth century American novels, but learns that this book is not on the recommended list, should not just be allowed to continue teaching *Moby Dick*, but should be applauded for doing so by an appreciative community. Whether it is *Moby Dick*, which is probably close to the official literature curriculum, or instruction in the life cycle of humming birds (my neighbors area of expertise and passion), or instruction about the Black jazz musicians who played baseball in France after WWI (my son's area of expertise) does not matter. I really do not much care if the teacher is an expert on mushrooms, airplanes, the Chicago Cubs, World War II, Turkish rugs, quilts, or aspects of physics, chemistry, biology, Photoshop, or number systems. What I care about is that teachers have fields they care about, understand deeply, and are provided the opportunity to teach what they know in depth and might love to teach, whether part of the "official" curriculum or not. Moreover, whatever the field, teachers could learn, over time, to "polish the stone." That is, teachers can make their curriculum of four or five hours, or for a few days each semester, nearly perfect introductions to the topics they love and know well. And, if a teacher does not really love anything that is broadly educational in or out of the official curriculum, they should go into the field of training, and leave the field of education to those who care deeply about knowledge in one or more areas.

I am convinced that were this done, students would prosper, teachers would have greater professional pride in their talents, schools would be places that are less impersonal, and broader conceptions of knowledge and skill would enhance our nations ability to face an uncertain future. Students and teachers deserve the opportunity to acknowledge and hear from those that possess expertise and they will profit from the gift of opportunity to instruct others in what they know deeply.

CONCLUSION

I am concerned with diversity of curriculum, diversity in conceptions of competence and success, diversity in assessment, and diversity in instruction. I am concerned that in high-stakes testing cultures such as the United States, the school curriculum is being narrowed. Although the intended curriculum (what state and local school boards want students to learn) is usually broad and well intended, the implemented curriculum (what happens in classrooms) is usually much more narrow, focused on the test. And, the achieved curriculum (what students actually learn) is more likely to be facts, ideas, names, dates and algorithms they have memorized, rather than the cognitive skills for engaging in critical thinking and problem solving.

The narrowing of the curriculum makes it quite likely that our students will get a distorted idea of who is smart, competent, and successful. Currently, they and their parents receive too limited a view of the nature of human talent. This limited view is hurtful to many students whose literacy and numeracy skills are not as high as desired by our schools, and whose special talents lay elsewhere.

The same high-stakes testing culture promotes use of multiple-choice items that possess a single right answer. But helping students to think critically and solve problems is our educational goal, and these desired outcomes of schooling cannot be assessed easily with assessments that rely almost exclusively on multiple-choice items.

Finally, I want to see a diverse curriculum infused with lively instruction in a wide variety of topics. Schools in test-oriented cultures are too often seen as boring by too many students. To elicit both a more diverse curriculum, with the possibility of more lively instruction, I suggest we make students into subject matter experts and communicators of their areas of expertise, and to give teachers the chance to teach that which they love.

The schools of the future need to think about their responses to cultural and linguistic diversity, issues that will not go away in our much more interdependent world. But educators cannot allow concern for diversity to stop there. Diversity in curriculum, conceptions of talent, assessment, and instruction need equal attention in a VUCA world. Increasing responsiveness to diversity in all these areas will promote a more adaptable, and thus a stronger nation.

REFERENCES

Berliner, D. C. (2011). Rational responses to high-stakes testing: The case of curriculum narrowing and the harm that follows. *Cambridge Journal of Education, 41*(3), 287–302.

Egan, K. (2010). *Learning in depth: A simple innovation that can transform schooling.* Chicago, IL: University of Chicago Press.

Johansen, B. (2007). *Get there early: Using foresight to provoke strategy and innovation.* San Francisco, CA: Berrett-Koehler Publishers.

CHAPTER 6

TEACH FREEDOM!

William Ayers
University of Illinois

ANALOGY TEST

High-stakes, standardized testing is to learning as:
  (a) memorizing a flight manual is to flying
  (b) watching Hawaii Five-O is to doing police work
  (c) exchanging marriage vows is to a successful marriage
  (d) reading Gray's Anatomy is to practicing surgery.
  (e) singing the national anthem is to good citizenship
  (f) all of the above

MULTIPLE CHOICE QUESTIONS

The typical American classroom has as much to offer an inquiring mind as does:
  (a) a vacant lot
  (b) a mall
  (c) a street corner
  (d) the city dump
  (e) the custodian's closet
  (f) none of the above

Schooling for Tomorrow's America, pages 73–81
Copyright © 2014 by Information Age Publishing
All rights of reproduction in any form reserved.

The answer to each is f, the first for obvious reasons, and the second because each of the others offers much more to an inquiring mind!

SCHOOLS: A REFLECTION OF SOCIETY

Schools serve society, and every society is reflected, for better and for worse, in its schools. Schools are in fact microcosms of the societies in which they're embedded, and every school is both mirror of and window into a specific social order. If one understands the schools deeply enough, one can see the whole of it; if one fully grasps the intricacies of society, one will know something about how its schools must be organized, and why.

In a totalitarian society, schools are built for obedience and conformity; in a kingdom, schools teach allegiance to the crown; an ancient agrarian community apprentices the young as full participants in a rustic world of farming; with a theocratic regime comes lessons in faithfulness and piety and devotion; under apartheid, schools inculcate an understanding that privilege and oppression are distributed along the color line. These schools might be "excellent" by some measures, but whatever else is taught—math or music, literature or science—the insistent curriculum looming over everything else is the big lessons of how to function *here and now in this specific social order*: the old South Africa had beautiful palaces of learning and small state-of-the-art classes for White kids, and overcrowded, dilapidated, and ill-equipped classes for the African kids, and that made perfect if perverse sense: apartheid schools mirrored an apartheid society, and everyone understood that hard, cruel fact. German schools in the middle of the twentieth century produced excellent scientists and athletes and artists and intellectuals, and they also produced submission and conformity, moral blindness and easy agreement, obtuse patriotism and a pathway straight into the furnaces.

Here and now, we are insistently encouraged to think of education as a product like a car or a refrigerator, a box of bolts or a screw driver—something bought and sold in the marketplace like any other commodity. The controlling metaphor for the schoolhouse is a business run by a CEO, with teachers as workers and students as the raw material bumping along the assembly line while information is incrementally stuffed into their little up-turned heads; it's rather easy to think within this model that "downsizing" the least productive units, "outsourcing" and privatizing a space that was once public is a natural event; that teaching toward a simple standardized metric, and relentlessly applying state-administered (but privately developed and quite profitable) tests to determine the "outcomes," is a rational proxy for learning; that centrally controlled "standards" for curriculum and teaching are commonsensical; that "zero tolerance" for student misbehavior as a stand-in for child development or justice is sane; and that "accountability," that is, a range of sanctions on students, teachers, and schools—but never on law-makers, foundations, corporations, or high officials—is logical and level-headed. This is in fact what a range of wealthy "reformers," noisy politicians, and their chattering pundits in the bought media call "school reform."

CHATTER ON SCHOOL REFORM

The magic ingredients for this reform recipe are three: replace the public schools with some sort of privately controlled administration; sort the winners relentlessly from the losers—*test*, test, TEST! (and then punish); and destroy teachers' ability to speak with any sustained and unified voice. The operative image for these moves has by now become quite familiar: education is an individual consumer good, not a public trust or a social good, and certainly not a fundamental human right. Management, inputs and outcomes, efficiency, cost controls, profit and loss—the dominant language of this kind of reform does not leave much room for doubt, or much space to breathe.

In this metaphoric strait-jacket, school learning is a lot like boots or hammers; unlike boots and hammers, the value of which is inherently satisfying and directly understood, the value of school learning is elusive and indirect. Its value, we're assured, has been calculated elsewhere by wise and accomplished people, and these school masters know better than anyone what's best for *these* kids (for other people's children) and for the world. "Take this medicine," students are told repeatedly, day after tedious day; "It's good for you." Refuse the bitter pill, and go stand in the corner—where all the other losers are assembled.

Schools for compliance and conformity are characterized by passivity and fatalism and infused with anti-intellectualism and irrelevance. They turn on the little technologies for control and normalization—the elaborate schemes for managing the mob, the knotted system of rules and discipline, the exhaustive machinery of schedules and clocks, the laborious programs of sorting the crowd into winners and losers through testing and punishing, grading, assessing, and judging, all of it adding up to a familiar cave, an intricately constructed hierarchy—everyone in a designated place and a place for everyone. In the schools as they are, here and now, knowing and accepting one's pigeonhole on the towering and barren cliff becomes the only lesson one really needs. And this model may be perfect for a society at the end of empire, bent on permanent war and experiencing the fatal eclipse of the public square.

When the aim of education is the absorption of facts, learning becomes exclusively and exhaustively selfish, and there is no obvious social motive for learning. The measure of success is always a competitive one. People are turned against one another, and every difference becomes a potential deficit. Getting ahead of others is the primary goal in such places, and mutual assistance, which can be so natural in other human affairs, is severely restricted or banned.

On the other hand, where active work is the order of the day, helping others is not a form of charity, something that impoverishes both recipient and benefactor. Rather, a spirit of open communication, interchange, and analysis becomes commonplace. In these places there is a certain natural disorder, a certain amount of anarchy and chaos, as there is in any busy workshop. But there is a deeper discipline at work, the discipline of getting things done and learning through life.

The education we've become accustomed to is simply a caricature—it's neither authentically nor primarily about full human development. Why, for example, is education thought of as only kindergarten through 12th grade, or kindergarten through university? Why does education occur only early in life? Why is there a point in our lives when we no longer think we need education? Why, again, is there a hierarchy of teacher over students? Why are there grades and grade levels? Why does attendance matter? Why is punctuality valuable? Why, indeed, do we think of a productive and a service sector in our society, with education designated as a service activity? Why is education separate from production?

The forces fighting to create the new common-sense—*school-reform-normal*— are led by a merry band of billionaires—Bill Gates, Michael Bloomberg, Sam Walton, Eli Broad—who work relentlessly to take up all the available space, preaching, persuading, and promoting, always spreading around massive amounts of cash to underline their fundamental points: dismantle public schools, crush the teachers unions, test, and punish. When Rupert Murdoch was in deep water in the summer of 2011, it came to light that Joel Klein, a leading "reformer" as head of the New York City public schools for years (and whose own kids, of course, attend private schools), was on Murdoch's payroll; according to the *New York Times*, (Peters, Barbaro, & Hernandez, 2011) the two saw eye to eye "on a core set of education principles: that charter schools needed to expand; poor instructors (the now-famous "lazy incompetent teachers") should be weeded out; and the power of the teachers union must be curtailed." These "marketeers" want to create a certain kind of schooling as part of a particular social vision.

EDUCATION: AN AREA OF STRUGGLE AND HOPE

Those of us who resist that particular narrow and anemic vision—who enter the contested space intent on fighting for more democracy, more joy and justice, and more peace and freedom—and who hope to live in a more emancipated society, struggle to create and nurture free schools. In a vibrant and liberated culture, schools would make an iron commitment to free inquiry, open questioning, and full participation; access and equity and simple fairness; a curriculum that encourages independent thought and judgment; and a base-line standard of complete recognition of the humanity of each individual. As opposed to obedience and conformity, the foundational curriculum would promote initiative, courage, imagination, and creativity. In other words, schools in an authentic and animated democracy would put the highest priority on the creation of free people geared toward enlightenment and liberation.

Education is always an arena of struggle as well as hope: struggle, because it stirs in us the need to look at the world anew, to question what we have created, and to wonder what is worthwhile for human beings to know and experience; and hope, because we gesture toward the future, toward the impending, toward the coming of the new. Education is where we ask how we might engage, enlarge, and change our lives, and it is, then, where we confront our dreams and fight out notions of the good life, where we try to comprehend, apprehend, or possibly even transform the world. What does it mean to be human in the twenty-first Century? Education is contested space, a natural site of conflict—sometimes restrained, other times in full eruption—because it raises the most fundamental questions.

The development of free people is the central goal of teaching toward a future free society. Teaching toward freedom and democracy is based on a *common faith in the incalculable value of every human being*, and acts on the principle that the fullest development of all is the condition for the full development of each, and, conversely, that the fullest development of each is the condition for the full development of all.

The democratic ideal has policy implications, of course, but it is deeply implicated as well in questions of teaching and curriculum. We expect schools in a democratic society to be defined by a spirit of *cooperation, inclusion, and full participation*, places that honor diversity while building unity. Schools in a democracy resist the overspecialization of human activity, the separation of the intellectual from the manual, the head from the hand, and the heart from the brain, the creative and the functional. The standard is *fluidity of function*, the variation of work and capacity, the *mobilization of intelligence and creativity and initiative and work in all directions*.

On the side of a liberating and humanizing education is a *pedagogy of questioning*, an approach that opens rather than closes the process of thinking, comparing, reasoning, perspective-taking, and dialogue. It demands something upending and revolutionary from students and teachers alike: Repudiate your place in the pecking order, it urges, remove that distorted, congenial mask of compliance: *You must change!*

We embrace the *importance of dialogue* with one another, and dialogue, as well, with a rich and varied past and a dynamic, unfolding future. In dialogue one speaks with the possibility of being heard, and simultaneously listens with the possibility of being changed. Dialogue is both the most hopeful and the most dangerous pedagogical practice, for in dialogue our own dogma and certainty and orthodoxy must be held in abeyance, must be subject to scrutiny.

The ethical core of teaching toward tomorrow is necessarily designed to create hope and a sense of agency and possibility in students. The big lessons are these: *history is still in-the-making,* the future unknown and unknowable, and what you do or don't do will make a difference (and of course choosing to not choose is itself a choice); *each of us is a work-in-progress*—unfinished, dynamic, in-process, on the move and on the make—swimming through the wreckage toward a distant and indistinct shore; *you don't need anyone's permission to interrogate the world.*

Teachers with freedom on their minds must recognize that the opposite of moral is indifferent, and that the opposite of aesthetic is anesthetic—they create then a range of aesthetic and ethical spaces for students to become engaged participants and not passive observers of life, and they open ground where everyone can wake up, open their eyes, and pay attention free of the blinders of ideology or habit. Students are encouraged to see it all, the splendor and the horror, to be astonished at both the loveliness of life and all the undeserved harm and pain around us, and then to release their social imaginations in order to act on behalf of what the known demands.

The challenging intellectual and ethical work of teaching pivots on our ability to see the world as it is, and simultaneously to see our students as three-dimensional creatures—human beings much like ourselves—with hopes and dreams, aspirations, skills, and capacities; with minds and hearts and spirits; with embodied experiences, histories, and stories to tell of a past and a possible future; with families, neighborhoods, cultural surrounds, and language communities all interacting, dynamic, and entangled. This knotty, complicated challenge requires patience, curiosity, wonder, awe, and more than a small dose of humility. It demands sustained focus, intelligent judgment, inquiry, and investigation. It calls forth an open heart and an inquiring mind since every judgment is contingent, every view partial, and each conclusion tentative.

Parents, students, and citizens, teachers and educators, might press now for an education worthy of a democracy and essential to a free people, including an end to sorting people into winners and losers through expensive standardized tests that act as pseudo-scientific forms of surveillance; an end to starving schools of needed resources and then blaming teachers and their unions for dismal outcomes; an end to the militarization of schools, "zero tolerance" policies, gender identity discrimination; and an end to "savage inequalities" and the rapidly accumulating "educational debt," the resources due to communities historically segregated, poorly funded and under-served. All children and youth in a democracy, regardless of economic or social circumstance, deserve full access to richly resourced classrooms led by caring, thoughtful, fully qualified, and generously compensated teachers.

LIBERATION PEDAGOGY: A NEW DIRECTION

All free people deserve Freedom Schools and Freedom School thinking in every classroom, school, community, or public space. We should re-ignite our democratic dreams, and mobilize to change what is clearly in our hands to change. We are not allowed to sit quietly in a democracy awaiting salvation from above. We are all equal, and we need to speak up and speak out about a new transformative educational practice serving the needs of a more peaceful and balanced, joyful and just community.

We must become bolder, more confident, and more creative in re-imagining school. Our biggest mistake is holding back, becoming cautious, and finding the familiarity of our failures too comfortable to throw off. Audacity! Audacity! Audacity! If schools are to become vibrant centers of intellectual and social growth, they must catch up with the cultural discourse which has had to locate outside, in the streets, the independent programs, and the new digital media spaces. We must build an education no one has to recover from.

We turn to the themes of liberation pedagogy: students become the subjects and the actors in constructing their own educations, not simply the objects of a regime of discipline and punishment; education becomes uncoupled from the inadequate and illegitimate meritocracy model and the public good becomes understood more fundamentally. Instead of schooling-as-credentialing, sorting, gate-keeping, and controlling, education enables *all* students to become smarter, more capable of negotiating our shared and complex world, more able to work effectively in community and across communities to innovate and initiate with courage and creativity. We all begin to re-examine core personal and ethical values in order to make more thoughtful, caring, and productive life choices. This requires courage—from teachers, families, communities, and students—to build alternative and insurgent classrooms and schools and community spaces focused on that we know we need rather than what we are told we must endure. Education, then, is transformed from rote boredom and endlessly alienating routines into something that is eye-popping and mind-blowing—always opening doors and opening minds and opening hearts as they forge their own pathways into an expansive world.

This is the urgency: "Generations do not cease to be born, and we are responsible to them because we are the only witness they have," writes the dazzling James Baldwin. "The sea rises, the light fails, lovers cling to each other, and children cling to us. The moment we cease to hold each other, the moment we break faith with one another, the sea engulfs us and the light goes out." This is the burning imperative for school people, parents, and residents today, and might become the measure of our determination now.

The schools we need—and schools that we can fight for now—are *lived in the present tense.* The best preparation for a meaningful future life is living a meaningful present life, and so rich experiences and powerful interactions—as opposed to school as a bitter pill—are on offer every day. A good school is *an artist's studio and a workshop for inventors,* a place where experimentation with materials and investigations in the world are an everyday happening. A good school is *fearless, risk-taking, thoughtful, activist, intimate, and deep,* a space where fundamental questions are pursued to their furthest limits.

Foundational questions that free people pursue might become the central stuff of our schools:

- What's your story?
- How is it like or unlike the stories of others?
- What do we owe one another?
- What does it mean to be human in the twenty-first Century?
- How can we become more human?
- What qualities and dispositions and knowledge are of most value to humanity?
- How can we nourish, develop, and organize full access to those valuable qualities?
- Why are we here?
- What do we want?
- What kind of world could we reasonably hope to create?
- How might we begin?

These questions—themes in literature and the arts through the ages—are critical, but they are not as lofty and distant as they might sound. In a preschool a teacher organizes a "Me Curriculum" and interviews each child over time, creating a section of wall devoted to a "Kid of the Week" where each is spotlighted telling the story of her family and how she got her first name, favorite books and food, and more. In a third grade, students interview a "Family Hero" and present oral histories to the group focused on significant events, migration or movement from place to place, and life-lessons learned.

A group of middle-school students in small groups choose an area for a year-long inquiry—an "I-search"—and explore the environment of the neighborhood mapping everything from housing and labor patterns to health and recreation and crime statistics. And high school kids work to develop a rich and varied portfolio for graduation—a set of works to be defended in front of a committee consisting of an advisor, a peer, a teacher, a community resident, and a family member—consisting of grades and test scores, of course, plus a huge range of other indicators of a productive high school learning experience: an original work of art, a physical challenge set and met, a favorite piece of writing, a record of community service, a work/study plan for the next four years, a list of the ten best books ever read, a reading autobiography projected five years forward, an essay on "What Makes an Educated Person," and so on.

Knowledge is an inherently *public* good—something that can be reproduced at little or no cost, and, like love, is generative: the more you have, the better off you become; the more you give away, the more you have. Offering knowledge and learning and education to others diminishes nothing. In a flourishing democracy, knowledge would be shared without any reservation or restrictions whatsoever. This points us toward an education that could be, but is not yet, an education toward full human development—humanization—enlightenment and freedom.

REFERENCE

Peters, J. W., Barbaro, M., Hernandez, J. C. (2011, July 23). Ex-schools chief emerges an unlikely Murdoch ally. *New York Times*. Retrieved from www.nytimes.com/2011/07/24/business/media/joel-klein-ex-school-chief-leads-internal-new-corp-inquiry.html?pagewanted=all

CHAPTER 7

WHAT MIGHT SCHOOLS OF THE FUTURE BE LIKE?

Deborah Meier
Steinhardt School of Education

Some days I wish I could come back in a half century and see what is going on in the world. On other days, I am glad I won't be able to do that. But some of those reading these words will perhaps be around, so here is some sage advice.

There are as many possible futures as we can imagine. We make the future as we go—out of all those possibilities in struggle with each other. I happen to be one of those who has had a chance over and over to bring to life my "dream" schools—although always compromised happily by the people I worked with—kids, parents, and teachers as well as by the realities of the present, including our internalized expectations, dreams, and fears, not to mention our sometimes false memories of what "used to be."

Thus, we need to ask ourselves what it is we want from schools. I waver between two related but not synonymous goals. First, that our schools help the young become adults who can nourish the ideas and practices of democracy—with a focus on the crises facing democracy at any particular moment! To do that, a democratic people must believe that the future has not yet been decided. Learning this is a central role of schooling *for* democracy.

Schooling for Tomorrow's America, pages 83–88

Second, that schooling should enhance every single child's sense of his/her own individual passions, entitlements, and strengths; and make it hard for others to discourage their dreams. Third, that they are in the habit of building strong, and respectful relationships with others, even others different from themselves.

So, let me put my cards on the table. I think we have lately taken a leap backwards from schooling *for* democracy, for passion and for strong personal bonds between people. The future I want to encourage requires at least three things: Healthy informed skepticism; the habit of empathy, especially when it's uncomfortable; and playfulness, "pretending," being accustomed to imagining otherwise. All three have been expelled from our schools, even play for very young children.

WHAT COULD BE DONE?

We could have:

1. Schools in which at least the adults have a voice and even a vote; today, we are placing decisions further and further away from them. In my dreams, schools' decisions are made by all those most concerned, within parameters comfortable to the larger political community and in keeping with the Constitution.
2. Democracy demands being "in the habit" of acknowledging the possibility that we are wrong! In fact, we are increasingly teaching children that the *only* thing of importance is getting the one right answer out of four. From bottom to top, schools must be designed to allow for dissent, to celebrate a good argument.
3. Democracy requires us to listen carefully. Meanwhile, more and more schools are being urged to adopt "no excuses" policies. In short, *don't* listen to wrong-doers or wrong thinkers. Opportunities in schools for the future must create myriad opportunities for listening, not just telling.
4. Democracy lives off a sense of shared and common dreams, with all the compromises this occasionally requires. However, the privatization of our schools is creating more and more barriers between the lucky and the unlucky. (Example; lotteries are a counter-intuitive way to instill a sense of hopefulness—when it all depends on the roll of the dice.)

Winston Churchill once said something like this: democracy is a thoroughly flawed idea, except if you consider the alternatives. It's greatest flaw, the mal-distribution of power, lies outside of school, but is fixable The top

2% of our citizens can too easily usurp the democratic process, make a run around it, via the power of their extraordinary financial resources.

Democracy, however, suggests an alternate source of power: people's voices, ideas, and the ballot box; and, schools are what make this possible—no matter how unlikely. Even Jefferson's clarion call for democracy for all was framed within a context in which "all" precluded women, people of color (slaves), and in many cases people who did not own property.

So, my dreams for the future schools will introduce the young to a range of possibilities for living the good life, they will create more potentially troublemaking citizens—capable of making sense of their own needs and the obstacles facing them, prepared to listen on the chance they may be wrong, prepared to revise their own opinions and strategies as they go through life and prepared to act on their convictions. And, finally, schools that teach the power of solidarity as well as that of the lonely holdout.

Habits are hard to come by. We all know *how* to put our keys away so that we can find them the next day. But we don't always *do it*. Habits become habitual by being over-practiced. So, the habits of the heart and mind of democracy must be over-practiced. Schools must be filled with adults who are practicing them in front of and with children. This means important decisions must be made collaboratively, *close* to the ground—by and for the students and those who have most at stake in their education.

THE MISSION HILL SCHOOL MODEL

At Mission Hill School in Boston, of which I was once a part, large-scale policy decisions were made by a school governing board consisting of equal numbers of family members, staff, and older students—plus members of the larger community co-opted by the other three constituents. However, no critical decision could be made, above all the selection of leaders, change of mission, and organizational structure, without the support of at least three out of five members of each constituency. Meanwhile, the organizing structure acknowledged the faculty's responsibility to prepare and submit a budget, a staffing plan, any changes in its curriculum design and assessment practices annually to the large governing body. If it was not accepted, the faculty was required to go back and revise it until a majority of each constituency was on board. Given current realities, the State and Local Boston governors could over-rule our work; but we pretended it could not and would not so decide!

In the areas designed for faculty autonomy the faculty members met regularly and designed a four year curriculum plan, revisited annually and implemented with a great deal of individuality within each classroom. But even within each classroom, although each teacher had freedom, we agreed that what we did was everyone's business. Consequently, each of us was open to criticism, and to peer review. The principal had power only as one member of a review team, with the right to veto decisions that he/she believed put us at financial risk or put children's health and safety at risk. Even these vetoes could be over-ruled, and appealed to the Board and or a mediator. In 15 years, not one veto was appealed or over-ruled; verifying the strength of this process.

Our classes were multi-aged. In part to make it easier for all teachers to get to know well all their students and their families; and considerable time was set aside for both collegial self-governance and for building relationships with families. We paid our teachers "extra" for these additional responsibilities with professional development funds allocated by the district, or special grants when we could find them. All these levels of discourse, argument, and exploration were open to everyone (except for some sessions dealing with personnel conversations involving individual students or staff).

We wanted students to see us in action not only among our students, but among our peers, their families and other teachers. This idea, at its source, is the common sense one: the young are most efficiently raised in the company of adults. Experts at adulthood have the best chance of preparing novices for becoming adults. It helped to keep our community small. Somewhere between 100 and 300 individuals probably works best in such a situation. Thus, the adults involved in decisions-making could, over and over again, gather together around one large table and "hear-out" each other; and where the number of classrooms did not prohibit all involved from becoming familiar with what children were experiencing in class, and the kind of work that was being produced in these classrooms. It also meant that every candidate's graduation "credentials" were available to one and all, and the Faculty voted that a student was graduation-ready based on a commonly agreed upon set of standards met.

This model is, however, only one of many that take seriously building a school to human scale so that young human beings could, over time, internalize its values, and question its faults. In short, the school's students could imagine how they might do it better if and when.... Not to mention that they were involved in suggesting changes in the here and now.

When it comes to examining the data at large, experts have discovered that none of the latest reform fads work if brought to scale—that is mandated for all. Not even for test scores (such a paltry notion of success) demonstrates one-best-way. If we rest our case on test scores alone it would be best to only accept well-to-do children whose families have advanced degrees. But for many of the values of Mission Hill (and other schools like it), wealth may or may not be an advantage. That's a freeing thought. It makes it easier to acknowledge that focusing on "test prep" is cheating the kids.

How better to introduce children to the larger world in direct and meaningful ways than to expose them to other views best expressed by other people, and to interesting vocations that might become central to their lives, but not present among the staff. These conditions also must be tackled. We did so at Mission Hill, but some schools have gone much further than we have in breaking the barriers between school and society. So have other schools broken more barriers between academic disciplines even as students get closer to graduating from 12th grade. But what such schools can do now, and someday—when Federal, State and Local policies are more tolerant, perhaps even encouraging, of such changes—will be the work of each school. They will benefit from keeping records of their work, meeting frequently with their graduates over many years, bringing in friends and enemies to provide feedback, and have the time to visit other schools. How grand it would be if large-scale data were available and could be trusted; however, at present we have very little reason to trust the data we like or the data we don't like, those that support "our kind" of reforms or those that support quite opposite kinds of reforms!

Meanwhile, we need to push the envelope as far as possible, and perhaps, a little further than we professionals are permitted even as we initiate conversations with one and all about the future for which we hope, as well as the schools that will make it easier to get there.

FINAL THOUGHTS

We have yet to work out all the ways this can happen. Nevertheless, we do know that centralizing authority more and more, distant from ourselves, especially through governmental authorities far removed from our site of operations, reduces, the odds for the kind of feisty citizenry that democracy requires. To be sure, these new schools will require studying history in ways that help us distinguish a true analogy from a false one, translating the blitz of statistics thrown in our face, knowing when not to rely on Science, with a great big capital S, and thirsting to live more lives than we have time for—by joining the stories of others through literature; and more and more.

Our Task

We need to:

1. Create more equal life conditions for others while also fighting to keep the public—you and I—in the center of public education.
2. Stop looking for the answers from others on matters in which we (you and I) are the best experts, e.g., our own child's ability to read,

especially looking at results from a test about which you know nothing and whose error of measurement is *huge* for any one individual.

3. Stop looking for the answer to what is the "best" curriculum by appointing distant experts to decide this *once and for all* for everyone. Remember: such experts change their minds at least as often as you and I do, and most have never tried to practice what they mandate for others. Nor is any child "average" in their needs at the moment or their desires for the future.

4. Stop assessing your child's teacher based on their student's test scores—thus confounding one mistake with more of them! Actually, as a parent, I first asked myself whether the teacher seemed to like my kids. Maybe that was a good place to start.

Finally, with open minds, parents and teachers must strive together for what their hearts and experiences tell them is best for the children and pupils they care for and about on a dialy basis.

CHAPTER 8

PREPARING TEACHERS
FOR TOMORROW'S AMERICA

Marilyn Cochran-Smith
Christine Power
Boston College

Preparing teachers for the challenges of diversity is one of the most pressing and complex challenges we face in creating schools for tomorrow's
America and indeed for tomorrow's global society. This chapter makes the
case for why this is such a critical challenge in terms of the convergence of
two global trends in demographics and policy attention to teacher quality. Then we describe and illustrate five major ways that teacher education
programs and projects across the country are working to prepare teachers
for diversity.

THE CONVERGENCE OF TWO GLOBAL TRENDS

In many nations throughout the world, there is increasing diversity in the
school population as well as increasing recognition of the challenges posed
by diversity (Banks, 2009; Castles, 2009; Organization for Economic Cooperation and Development, 2006). In the United States, there have been

Schooling for Tomorrow's America, pages 89–106
Copyright © 2014 by Information Age Publishing
All rights of reproduction in any form reserved.

enormous increases in immigration over the last decade, bringing large numbers of students whose first language is not English into the public schools and as well as a heightened awareness of diversity. This has added to a situation where inequities based on the marginalization of indigenous and formerly enslaved minorities have been emphasized since the Civil Rights movements of the 1960s and 1970s (Banks, 2009).

However, even in countries that have long been considered homogeneous in language, ethnicity and culture, the situation has changed (Banks, 2009; Castles, 2009). In Japan, for example, the current trend is that there are more people coming in to the country than going out. This includes Japanese returnees as well as newcomers from African and South American countries (Hirasawa, 2009). In Scotland, there have been increases in the overall population due to immigration increases for the last several years. Of course, the number of immigrants to places like Scotland and Japan is far smaller than the number of immigrants to the United States or to some European countries (Hossain, 2007), but the trend is in the same direction. Globally, these new patterns of immigration have brought new attention to the challenges posed by diversity and of the inequities in achievement and other school-related outcomes that persist between majority and minority groups in many nations (May, 2009).

At the same time that we have increased diversity in the school population in many nations around the world, there is another important global trend. There is now unprecedented emphasis on teacher quality in most nations with extremely high expectations for teacher performance (Cochran-Smith, 2005; Furlong, Cochran-Smith & Brennan, 2009). Based on the assumption that education and the economy are tightly linked, it is now assumed in many countries that teachers can—and should—teach all students to world-class standards, serve as the linchpins in educational reform, and produce a well-qualified labor force to preserve or boost a nation's position in the global economy (Darling-Hammond, 2010; McKenzie & Santiago, 2005). In short, globally, teachers have been identified as one of the major determinants, if not the key factor, in the quality of education, which in turn is tied to the economic health of nations (OECD, 2005).

Our major point here is that in the first decade of the twenty-first century, these two trends have converged-heightened attention to the increasing diversity of the school population and unprecedented emphasis on teachers as the key factor in educational quality. The result is that teachers are now expected to play a major role in meeting the challenges of a diverse globalized society by ensuring that all school students have both rich learning opportunities and equitable learning outcomes.

THE DEMOGRAPHIC IMPERATIVE

In this chapter, we concentrate on the challenges of preparing teachers to work with increasingly diverse student populations in the U.S. context. Some people have used the phrase, "the demographic imperative" (Banks, 1995; Dilworth, 1992) or the "demographic divide" (Gay & Howard, 2000) to describe the current U.S. educational context with regard to diversity. The racial and ethnic characteristics of the school population in the United States have changed dramatically over the last several decades—from 78% of White students (i.e., from European American backgrounds) and 22% students of color (i.e., African-American, Hispanic, Asian, or indigenous Native American) in 1972 to 55% White students and 45% students of color in 2008 (National Center for Education Statistics, 2003, 2010a). Demographers predict that by 2035, the majority of school students in the United States will be from these minority groups (Hodgkinson, 2002).

Another way to think of the diversity in U.S. schools is in terms of the number of those whose first language is not English—often referred to in U.S. schools as English language learners, but preferably referred to as "multilingual learners" to emphasize multiple language capacity as a strength not a deficit. The number of multilingual learners increased from 3.8 million in 1979 to 10.9 million almost 20 years later (National Center for Education Statistics, 201 0b). In addition, the number of students with disabilities who receive special education services, many of whom spend much of their time in regular education classrooms, increased from just over 4 million in 1981 to more than 6.5 million in 2008 (National Center for Education Statistics, 2009).

We want to make it very clear here that we are not suggesting that diversity itself is a problem. In fact, as teacher educators, we see diversity as an asset rather than a problem or a deficit, and we value diversity as a benefit in a pluralistic society and in a democracy, a point we elaborate on below. But there are severe and important disparities related to diversity. Commonly referred to as "the achievement gap," it is now widely known that there are marked disparities among the achievement levels of student groups that differ from one another racially, culturally, linguistically, socioeconomically, and geographically (Ladson-Billings, 2006). Specifically, it is now well documented that White and Asian students consistently score higher than their African-American and Hispanic counterparts on standardized tests of reading and mathematics skills. African-Americans and Hispanics also have higher rates of dropping out of high school and lower rates of high school graduation and college attendance than White and Asian students. This, then, is the "demographic imperative"—the urgent need to reduce the persistent association between demographic diversity, on one hand, and disparities in school achievement and other outcomes, on the other hand (Economic Policy Institute, 2008).

Of course, it is critical to ask what explains this, although this is an extraordinarily complex question. Some of the explanation—in fact, a great deal of this—surely has to do with high poverty levels for many minority groups and with the long and unfortunate history of racism in our country (Berliner, 2005; Rothstein, 2004). We believe strongly, along with others in the United States (e.g., Economic Policy Institute, 2008), that we will never solve the problem of the demographic divide unless we decrease poverty and racism and increase the social and economic resources of all students and their families. But this is a topic for a whole different chapter—many of them, in fact. What we want to concentrate on in this chapter is another aspect of the problem—the part of the problem that has to do with teachers, teaching, and teacher preparation.

In the United States, there is a stark difference in the demographic profile of the student population and the demographic profile of teachers. Although the student population has become increasingly diverse, as we indicated above, the teacher population continues to be primarily White, European American, middle class, and monolingual (Villegas & Lucas, 2004). Like the issue of diversity itself, the fact that teachers and students are different from one another demographically is not in and of itself a problem, but there are problems associated with this. There are marked differences in the biographies and experiences of many teachers who are White European American from middle-class backgrounds who speak only English, on the one hand, and the many students who are people of color, or who live in poverty, or speak a first language that is not English, on the other hand. Geneva Gay (1993), for example, has found that many White monolingual teachers tend not to have the same cultural frames of reference and points of view as their students of color because they live in what she calls "different existential worlds." The result is that, unless they are specifically prepared to do otherwise and supported in trying to do otherwise, many White teachers have difficulty functioning as role models for students of color or acting as cultural brokers who help students bridge home-school differences (Goodwin, 2000).

We also know that, without specific support and instruction, many majority teachers have difficulty constructing curriculum, instruction, and assessments that are culturally responsive (Ladson-Billings, 1999). Perhaps, most serious—unless they have powerful teacher education experiences that help them do otherwise and unless they have ongoing support—many White middle-class teachers understand diversity as a deficit to be overcome and tend to have lower expectations for students who are different from themselves, especially those in urban areas (Irvine, 1990; Villegas & Lucas, 2001).

We want to add some detail to this statistical picture about the diversity challenges faced by new teachers. Along with colleagues at Boston College, we have been studying how people learn to teach over time, beginning with systematic examination of their experience in the teacher education program and then continuing into their early years of teaching (Cochran-Smith, Shakman, et al., 2009; Cochran-Smith, Gleeson & Mitchell, 2010; McQuillan, D'Souza, et al., 2009).

Here is the situation of one teacher in our study, Elizabeth Sigel.[1] Her name has been changed here, but all of the details of her situation are true. Elizabeth is a White European American young woman who attended well-resourced suburban schools with a primarily White population. During her first year as a high school English teacher, she taught four different courses per day with 25–30 different students in each. The student population was 94% African-American or Hispanic, 62% of whom were low income, 35% spoke English as a second language, and 18% had limited English proficiency. The school provided little data about students' backgrounds or language abilities. Multiple times during the year, new students arrived in class with no accompanying information regarding their academic strengths and weaknesses, learning disabilities, or English language mastery. Once, toward the end of the school year, a new student arrived from an African country, and Elizabeth realized after a brief conversation that he struggled greatly with spoken English and had even more limited writing abilities. She realized he would need considerable assistance in every area, yet she also worried about the fact that she had more than 100 other students who also needed support.

A second teacher from our study, Sylvie Lee, is a Chinese-American woman and a native speaker of Mandarin. Her first teaching job was in an urban elementary school in the heart of Boston's Chinatown district. 70% of the students in her school did not speak English as their primary language at home and 50% of all students were identified as not proficient in English. 11% of the school population was African-American, and another 11% was Hispanic. 82% of the students lived at or below the poverty level, with many immigrant parents working in low paying restaurant positions. 17% of the students had been identified as having learning disabilities. Sylvie's language skills were essential in working with the many students coming directly from mainland China with no English experience, but her students' language backgrounds also included Cantonese, Japanese (from Argentina), and Korean. Some of the children in her classes had just arrived in the country, while others still struggled with literacy skills after several years as residents. A third teacher from our study, Flick Webb, is a White male who teaches English in a public charter school in Boston. Flick's school was 72% low income, with 93% students of color, 36% English language learners, and another 3% identified as limited English proficiency.

PREPARING TEACHERS
FOR THE CHALLENGES OF DIVERSITY

Our intention here with both the statistics about the demographics of U.S. schools and the details of the teaching settings of three first year teachers is to make the point that in teacher education, we face considerable challenges in providing the educational support teacher candidates need to provide the educational support diverse learners need. Across the teacher education community, many teacher education practitioners and researchers are working on preparing teachers for the challenges of diversity in a number of key ways, including: values, frameworks, mission statements, and standards focused on diversity; coursework about diversity, culture, race, and language; guided experiences in diverse/cross-cultural communities; well-supervised clinical experiences in diverse schools; and, recruitment of a diverse pool of teacher candidates. In the remainder of this chapter, we take up each of these individually, providing elaboration and selected examples.

Values, Frameworks, Mission Statements, and Standards About Diversity

A very important part of preparing teachers for the challenges of diversity is the development and implementation of shared values, conceptual frameworks, mission statements, and professional standards regarding diversity, equality, and equity, by national professional organizations and accreditors, state-level departments of education, and, individual higher education institutions and programs. These make a clear statement about what matters and what is valued. The American Association of Colleges for Teacher Education (AACTE) had a great deal of influence in this area. In the 1970s, it established the first Commission on Multicultural Education and issued a statement titled, "No One Model America," which included these words (Baptiste & Baptiste, 1980): "Multicultural education recognizes cultural diversity as a fact of life in American society, and it affirms that this cultural diversity is a valuable resource that should be preserved and extended" (p. 1).

The full AACTE statement made three key assertions:

1. Diversity is a valuable resource.
2. This resource ought to be preserved and extended rather than merely tolerated or made to "melt away."

3. A commitment to diversity and to cultural pluralism ought to permeate all aspects of teacher preparation (Baptiste & Baptiste, 1980).

By 1981, the National Council for the Accreditation of Teacher Education (NCATE) required that institutions seeking accreditation show evidence that they provided all teachers with knowledge and skills related to multicultural education (Gollnick, 1992).

Since that time, there have been many other statements reinforcing the commitment of professional teacher education organizations and accreditors to preparing teachers for diversity and valuing diversity as an asset, not a deficit. Our major point here is that values that are shared by the profession and made explicit in major statements and standards are important components of teacher preparation for diversity. This applies at the local institutional level as well. The most effective teacher preparation programs are highly coherent in terms of values related to diversity across coursework, fieldwork, and other learning opportunities. In an analysis of research related to preparation of teachers for multicultural classrooms, Christine Sleeter (2008) concluded that programs with the most internal coherence also had the strongest impact on the development of teachers' beliefs and practices.

At our own institution, Boston College, for example, we have for many years had as an over-arching theme for the preparation of teachers the idea of learning to teach for social justice, emphasizing that all educators are responsible for challenging inequities and working with others to establish a more just society. As part of that larger goal, the program has four explicit themes, several of which specifically addresses diversity, like this one: "We believe that one of the central challenges of teaching is meeting the needs of all learners, especially as the school population becomes more diverse in race, culture, ethnicity, language background, and ability/disability." This theme and the program's overarching goal of social justice education are stated on all of the program's course syllabi, program materials, website, and promotional literature.

The focus is to help teacher candidates understand diversity as an asset and to teach them how to build on students' cultural, linguistic, and experiential resources in the classroom. Of course, simply stating that something is important does not actually make it important in practice, and there are many challenges that the program continues to face. But there have been extensive faculty discussions about the meaning of these goals, and there have been multiple efforts to construct learning to teach for social justice as an outcome of teacher education using a variety of new assessment tools.

Coursework for Diversity

The second component of teacher preparation for diversity focuses on coursework that prepares teachers to work effectively with diverse populations. One of the most important things the teacher education community has learned about this is that these issues cannot simply be lumped together into one course, such as "the diversity course" as all the rest of the courses are left intact. Rather, issues of diversity must be integrated and infused throughout all coursework, (Zeichner, 1993) even courses about teaching mathematics or biology. This also means that addressing issues of diversity must be the responsibility of every teacher educator, not simply those designated as experts in this area (Villegas & Lucas, 2001).

There are a number of key ideas that teacher candidates are expected to learn in coursework. First—and perhaps foremost—teachers need to learn that diversity is an asset, not a deficit. Historically, in the United States, diversity has been constructed from a deficit perspective about the education of minority students, particularly African-Americans and Hispanics. Gloria Ladson-Billings (1999) has called this the "perversity of diversity" (p. 216) where White is normative and diversity is equated with disadvantage and deficiency. For many prospective teachers who are White and relatively privileged members of society, it is difficult not to see diversity as a deficit (Villegas & Lucas, 2001). Part of what coursework tries to do, then, is to interrupt the deficit perspectives that many teacher candidates bring with them.

This is related to a second aspect of coursework, which is rethinking and challenging certain assumptions about the educational system that are taken for granted, but do not support the educational needs of diverse students. One of these assumptions is the notion of meritocracy, or the idea that success in school is based solely on merit and hard work (Sleeter, 1995), which subtly reinforces the idea that failure for certain individuals or groups is "normal" (Goodwin, 2001). Another assumption to be challenged is the notion of "color blindness," or the idea that racism and other forms of oppression based on differences are old problems that have been solved (Gay & Howard, 2000). This is especially important now that we have a Black president in the United States. It is easy for some people to assume that we now live in a "color-blind" society. This is clearly not the case, but teachers need coursework that helps them understand.

A third assumption to be challenged in coursework is that a major purpose of schooling is assimilating all students into the mainstream (Grant & Wieczorek, 2000; Weiner, 1993). Instead, goals of pluralism are essential. This does not negate the goal of all school students learning English so they are well prepared for higher education and meaningful work and feel a sense of identity as participants in American democratic society. But with the goal of pluralism rather than assimilation, students also maintain their own cultural, language, and ethnic identities. Challenging dominant assumptions requires transformative learning experiences that interrupt common ideas about merit, oppression, and assimilation (Jenks, Lee, & Kanpol, 2001; Sleeter, 1995).

One of the most important things to be learned in coursework about diversity is knowledge and information about culture itself. In a text for prospective teachers, for example, Etta Hollins (1996) points out that "culture is the medium for cognitive learning for all human beings, not just ethnic minorities and low income children" (p. 71). This means that teachers need to have complex understandings of the deep meanings of culture, the impact of culture on learning and schooling, the ways schools and classrooms function as cultures, and the role of culture in patterns of socialization, interaction, and communication. Another very important part of what teachers learn in coursework is "cultural consciousness" (Gay & Howard, 2000; Villegas & Lucas, 2001); that is, thinking of themselves as cultural beings at the same time they learn positive attitudes toward students with different cultural backgrounds.

One example of how teacher education coursework accomplishes these goals is through the assignment of "cultural autobiography" in which teacher candidates examine their own backgrounds. For some candidates, this means realizing, for the first time, that they are not simply "regular" while others are diverse or cultural, but that they are instead, the product of particular socialization processes and experiences that are cultural and social. Finally, teachers need to learn in coursework how to be self-reflective to take an inquiry stance (Cochran-Smith & Lytle, 1999, 2009) on teaching and to have self-knowledge about teaching and learning.

Experiences in Cross-Cultural Communities

Of course, none of the cultural knowledge described in the preceding sections matters unless teachers know how to act on it to work effectively with diverse learners. The third and fourth components of teacher preparation for diversity have to do with action. The third component of teacher preparation for diversity is guided experiences in diverse, cross-cultural communities. The key word here is "guided" in that it is critical that community experiences are well-planned, thoughtfully carried out, and well-scaffolded in terms of teachers' learning (Melnick & Zeichner, 1996; Sleeter, 2008).

Through community experiences, teacher candidates learn in action and in concrete ways what it really means to say that diversity is an asset, not a deficit by learning about the values, knowledge traditions, strengths, priorities and contributions of diverse communities. This may happen by working overtime at least over a semester, perhaps a year or more as a tutor with a family literacy project, a volunteer in a school program for homeless children, a church- or community-sponsored project to provide aid to communities, or a soup kitchen for unemployed families (Cochran-Smith & Fries, 2005; Sleeter, 2008). This might also occur through the process of what are called "cultural immersion" experiences (Sleeter, 2008), which might be, for example, semester-long work in a school or community center on an American Indian reservation, or, for teacher candidates whose preparation program is located in suburban or small town areas, this might be a semester's work in an urban school, or an experience living and creating educational enrichment programs in a Mexican-American community. Some teacher preparation programs for diversity also require teacher candidates to conduct ethnographic studies in urban communities and schools to enhance their understandings about culture, attitudes, and expectations.

Cross-cultural community based learning experiences are intended to help teachers learn about a community that is culturally different from their own by spending guided time there. The "guided" part means that they are equipped with learning strategies in advance and with guidance about what to observe and how to interpret what they see and experience. The quality and extent of the learning depend on the quality and extent of reflection and reading that are connected to the community experience, the duration and quality of the experience itself, and the facilitation and support preservice teachers have as they make sense of the experiences.

For example, as part of the Ohio State University's teacher education program, Barbara Seidl and colleagues (Seidl & Friend, 2002) worked with members of a local African-American church to build a cross-cultural community experience that would enhance the learning of teacher candidates but also contribute to the work of the church.

Over a long period, teacher educators created an "equal-status, community-based" internship for teacher candidates. Candidates worked 2–3 hours a week alongside others in various after-school, extended care, tutoring, and social support programs run by the church. In each case, the teacher candidates were encouraged to observe, listen, and learn from the knowledge traditions and priorities of the community as well as support the children and adults within the program. Members of the church community and the OSU faculty met regularly with the candidates to mediate the experience and guide the work. The community internship was closely connected to coursework and fieldwork in the program.

Well-Supervised Fieldwork in Schools With Diverse Populations

The fourth component of teacher preparation for diversity is well-supervised, well-supported clinical experiences in diverse schools that are closely linked to coursework and other learning opportunities. The emphasis in these clinical experiences is on helping teacher candidates support the educational needs of diverse learners by engaging directly in practice and learning from practice. For example, teachers develop and learn to apply appropriate interpretive perspectives about what happens in schools and classrooms (Cochran-Smith, 1999, 2000). The assumption here is that practice is not simply what teachers *do* in classrooms, which can be prescribed and assessed independent of local communities and cultures and independent of the specific needs of diverse learners. Rather, practice also involves the idea that teachers think about their work and interpret what is going on and how they understand competing agendas, pose questions, and make decisions.

Of critical importance is that teachers develop cultural competence (Gay, 1993; Goodwin, 2000; Villegas & Lucas, 2001; Zeichner, 1993), which involves establishing and maintaining caring relationships with diverse students that support their learning. This also means learning to work respectfully and effectively with colleagues, families, communities and social groups. At the heart of all this is that teachers work from high expectations for all students, including those who speak languages different from the majority, those whose ethnic or cultural backgrounds differ from those of the teacher or from dominant groups, and those who have special needs. This can only happen in well managed classroom environments that are respectful of all students so that culturally appropriate curriculum, pedagogy and assessment can be provided. Responsive curriculum and pedagogy build on the cultural, linguistic and experiential resources that students bring to school. Responsive assessment is formative, embedded in instruction, and learning-centered.

Finally teachers need to learn specific practices for working with diverse students. For multilingual learners, who are sometimes recent immigrants and sometimes students who have been in schools for several years, this means ensuring that they gain language skills and also learn rich academic content (Lucas & Grinberg, 2008). For students with special needs, this means ensuring that they have access to the general curriculum through differentiated instruction and other specific strategies.

At our institution, for example, teacher candidates gain clinical experiences in the diverse school settings of the Boston area where 38% of students are multilingual learners, many of whose families are recent immigrants to the United States. These students come from 40 different countries with home languages including Spanish, Chinese, Cape Verdean Creole, Haitian Creole, and Vietnamese. The teacher preparation program focuses on fieldwork experiences that prepare all teachers to work with multilingual learners. For example, teacher candidates at the primary level learn how to read aloud to multilingual learners, while secondary candidates learn how to assess the language demands of their content areas, develop language objectives for every lesson, and provide opportunities for students to develop English literacy at the same time they learn subject matter knowledge. Both primary and secondary teacher candidates engage in research and reflection about their developing practices and receive specific feedback from supervisors about their practice.

Recruiting and Selecting a Diversified Pool of Teacher Candidates

The final component of teacher education for diversity has to do with the recruitment and selection of a diverse pool of teacher candidates and then drawing on their experiential and cultural resources for working with diverse populations. The intention here is to increase the overall diversity of the teacher workforce so that all students have role models in the classroom as well as teachers who have high-level learning expectations for them and who are effective in terms of their educational achievement (Villegas & Lucas, 2004). This happens through a variety of programs specifically aimed at recruiting teachers for urban schools or other high needs areas and also through special teacher preparation programs that recruit teachers from nontraditional pools, such as teacher aides or assistants, minority college graduates seeking a career change, and non-certified teachers. This approach has been particularly effective at increasing the diversity of the teaching force and providing fully qualified teachers for high-need areas (Clewell & Villegas, 2001; Villegas, et al., 1995).

It is especially important to recruit a diversified teacher work force with high expectations for students and attributes that make them likely to succeed in diverse settings. For example, we know that those who enter teaching with experience in diverse settings and communities tend to be more successful—and stay longer—in diverse schools. We also know that there is some evidence that teachers of color tend to have higher expectations for students of color and are more able to connect with them in terms of life experiences and cultural worlds (Irvine, 1990). For example, Martin Haberman's (Haberman & Post, 1998) teacher preparation program in Milwaukee, Wisconsin, has prepared teachers for low-income schools for many years. Haberman screens teacher candidates on the basis of the attributes of persistence, the extent to which they value student learning, ability to survive in a bureaucracy, and fallibility, which refers to how they deal with mistakes, because he has found that these are the attributes that are most important in working with this diverse population.

Finally, in recruiting and selecting a more diversified group of teacher candidates, it is important to draw on their cultural, experiential and linguistic resources (Villegas & Davis, 2008). Otherwise, they are much more likely to drop out of programs and never make it into the teaching force because they may feel alienated in programs primarily intended to serve the needs of White teacher candidates. Our point here is that although this is complicated, there are many important reasons why teacher preparation programs and pathways endeavor to diversify the teacher work force for the diverse student population.

CONCLUSION: PREPARING TEACHERS FOR TOMORROW'S AMERICA

Demographers suggest that tomorrow's America will not be like today's America. The nation will continue to attract large numbers of new immigrants, with Hispanics and Asians, many of whom are multilingual learners, the fastest growing groups (Hodgkinson, 2002; National Center for Education Statistics, 2007). More and more students with special needs and disabilities will be served in general education classrooms. More and more parents will demand that their children have not only equal opportunities to be taught by excellent teachers in well-resourced schools, but also equal outcomes in terms of achievement, high school graduation rates, readiness levels for higher education, and the knowledge and skills needed for meaningful work.

We already ask teachers to do everything from drug counseling to suicide prevention, job preparation to bully identification, at the same time they are expected to raise test scores, meet the needs of an incredibly diverse school population, and prepare the nation's labor force for global competition. It is likely that we will continue to have extremely high expectations for teachers.

To provide the teachers needed for tomorrow's schools, teacher education programs and pathways will need to redouble their efforts to do the kind of work we have described in this chapter. This can help, but it cannot fix everything. In addition to working to prepare teachers for the challenges of diversity, to meet the needs of tomorrow's America, we will need to recognize that although teachers can join with others to challenge inequities and work for school change, the dire circumstances of children living in poverty are not going to change simply because teachers teach better.

Along these lines, Weiner (1993) has asserted that the challenges of urban teaching are the result of systemic deficiencies that individual teachers cannot alter—complex school bureaucracies, the isolation of schools from the communities they are supposed to serve, and the large numbers of students whose families have neither the resources nor the will to support school values. The same critiques can be made about those who imply that teacher quality is the panacea for that which is wrong in today's schools and indeed with today's America. We need to prepare the very best teachers we can, but we cannot work with blinders on—with a singular focus on fixing society by enhancing teacher quality, which places enormous and unrealistic responsibility on individual teachers. Instead, we will need to work harder at preparing teachers at the same time that we put into place policies and programs that address larger systemic issues.

NOTES

1. Marilyn Cochran-Smith and Patrick McQuillan served as Co-Principal Investigators for the "Qualitative Case Studies" research project. Core researchers included: Joan Bamatt, Lisa D'Souza, Cindy Jong, Kara Mitchell, Karen Shakman, and Dianna Gahlsdof Terrell. The three examples mentioned here draw on case information compiled by Lisa D'Souza, Joan Bamatt, and Dianna Terrell, respectively.

REFERENCES

Banks, J. (1995). Multicultural education: Historical development, dimensions, and practice. In J. Banks & C. Banks (Eds.), *Handbook of research on multicultural education* (pp. 3–24). New York: Macmillan Publishing.

Banks, J. (2009). Multicultural education: Dimensions and paradigms. In J. Banks (Ed.), *The Routledge international companion to multicultural education* (pp. 9–32). New York: Routledge.

Baptiste, H., & Baptiste, M. (1980). Competencies toward multiculturalism. In H. Baptiste, M. Baptiste, & D. Gollnick (Eds.), *Multicultural teacher education: Preparing teacher educators to provide educational equity* (Vol. 1). Washington, DC: AACTE.

Berliner, D. (2005). Our impoverished view of educational reform. *Teachers College Record, 108*(6), 949–995.

Castles, S. (2009). World population movements, diversity, and education. In J. Banks (Ed.), *The Routledge international companion to multicultural education* (pp. 49–61). New York: Routledge.

Clewell, B., & Villegas, A. (2001). *Evaluation of the DeWitt Wallace-Reader's Digest Fund's pathways to teacher careers program.* New York: Wallace Reader's Digest Fund.

Cochran-Smith, M. (1999). Learning to teach for social justice. In G. Griffin (Ed.), *The education of teachers: Ninety-eighth yearbook of the National Society for the Study of Education* (pp. 114–144). Chicago: University of Chicago Press.

Cochran-Smith, M. (2000). Blind vision: Unlearning racism in teacher education. *Harvard Educational Review, 70*(2), 157–190.

Cochran-Smith, M. (2005). The new teacher education: For better or for worse? *Educational Researcher 34*(6), 181–206.

Cochran-Smith, M., & K. Fries (2011). Teacher quality, teacher education and diversity: Policy and politics. In A. Ball & C. Tyson, (Eds.). *Studying diversity in teacher education*. Washington, American Educational Research Association.

Cochran-Smith, M., Gleeson, A. M., & Mitchell, K. (2010). Teacher education for social justice: What's pupil learning got to do with it? *Berkeley Review of Education, 1*(1), Retrieved from: http:scholarship.org/uc/item/35v7b2rv

Cochran-Smith, M., & Lytle, S. (1999). Relationship of knowledge and practice: Teacher learning in communities. In A. Iran-Nejad & C. D. Pearson (Eds.), *Review of research in education* (Vol. 24, pp. 249–306). Washington, DC: American Educational Research Association.

Cochran-Smith, M., & Lytle, S. (2009). *Inquiry as Stance: Teacher research for the next generation*. New York: Teachers College Press.

Cochran-Smith, M., McQuillan, P., Bamatt, J., D'Souza, L., Jong, C., Shakman, K., et al. (2010). *Who's fit to teach: A longitudinal study of teaching practice and career trajectory*. Paper presented at the Annual Meeting of the American Educational Research Association, Denver, Colorado, April30, 2010.

Cochran-Smith, M., Shakman, K., Jong, C., Bamatt, J., Terrell, D., & McQuillan, P. J. (2009). Good and just teaching: The case for social justice in teacher education. *American Journal of Education, 115*(3), 3347–3377.

Darling-Hammond, L. (2010). *The flat world and education: How America's commitment to equity will determine our future*. New York: Teachers College Press.

Dilworth, M. E. (1992). *Diversity in teacher education: New expectations*. San Francisco: Jossey-Bass.

Economic Policy Institute (2008). *A broader, bolder approach to education*. Retrieved from http_:/fwww.boldapproac.lLQrg/.

Furlong, J., Cochran-Smith, M., & Brennan, M. (2009). (Eds.) *Policy and politics in teacher education: International perspectives*. London: Routledge, Taylor & Francis.

Gay, G. (1993). Building cultural bridges: A bold proposal for teacher education. *Education and Urban Society, 25*(3), 285–289.

Gay, G., & Howard, T. (2000). Multicultural teacher education for the 21st century. *The Teacher Educator, 36*(1), 1–16.

Goodwin, A. (2000). Teachers as (multi)cultural agents in schools. In R. Carter (Ed.), *Addressing cultural issues in organizations: Beyond the corporate context* (pp. 104–114). Thousand Oaks, CA: Sage.

Goodwin, A. (2001). Seeing with different eyes: Reexamining teachers' expectations through racial lenses. In S. King & L. Castenell (Eds.), *Racism and racial inequality: Implications for teacher education*. Washington, DC: AACTE.

Gollnick, D. (1992). Multicultural education: Policies and practices in teacher education. In C. Grant (Ed.), *Research and multicultural education: From the margins to the mainstream* (pp. 218–239). London: Falmer Press.

Grant, C., & Wieczorek, K. (2000). Teacher education and knowledge in "the knowledge society": The need for social moorings in our multicultural schools. *Teachers College Record, 102*(5), 913–935.

Haberman, M., & Post, L. (1998). Teachers for multicultural schools: The power of selection. *Theory into Practice, 37*(2), 96–104.

Hirasawa, Y. (2009). Multicultural education in Japan. In J. Banks (Ed.), *The Routledge international companion to multicultural education* (pp. 159–169). New York: Routledge.

Hodgkinson, H. (2002). Demographics and teacher education. *Journal of Teacher Education, 53*(2), 102–105.

Hollins, E. (1996). *Culture in school learning: Revealing the deep meaning.* Mahwah, NJ: Lawrence Erlbaum.

Hossain, F. (2007, June 22). Snapshot: Global migration. *The New York Times.* Retrieved from http://www.nytimes.com.

Irvine, J. (1990). *Black students and school failure.* New York, NY: Greenwood Press.

Jenks, C., Lee, J., & Kanpol, B. (2001). Approaches to multicultural education in preservice teacher education: Philosophical frameworks and models for teaching. *The Urban Review, 33*(2), 87–105.

Ladson-Billings, G. (1999). Preparing teachers for diverse student populations: A critical race theory perspective. In A. Iran-Nejad & D. Pearson (Eds.), *Review of research in education* (Vol. 24, pp. 211–248). Washington, DC: American Educational Research Association.

Ladson-Billings, G. J. (2006). From the achievement gap to the education debt: Understanding achievement in U.S. schools. *Education Researcher, 35*(7), 3–12.

Lucas, T., & Grinberg, J. (2008). Responding to the linguistic reality of mainstream classrooms: Preparing all teachers to teach English language learners. In M. Cochran-Smith, S. Feiman Nemser, J. Mcintyre, & K. Demers (Eds.), *Handbook of research on teacher education (3rd edition): Enduring questions in changing contexts* (pp. 606–636). New York: Routledge, Taylor and Francis.

May, S. (2009). Critical multiculturalism and education. In J. Banks (Ed.), *The Routledge international companion to multicultural education.* (pp. 33–48). New York: Routledge.

McKenzie, P., & Santiago, P. (2005). *Teachers matter: Attracting, developing and retaining effective teachers.* Paris: Office for Economic Cooperation and Development.

McQuillan, P. J., D'Souza, L. A., Scheopner, A., Miller, G., Gleeson, A. M., Mitchell, K., & Cochran-Smith, M. (2009) Reflecting on pupil learning to promote social justice: A Catholic university's approach to assessment. *Catholic Education: A Journal of Inquiry and Practice, 13*(2), 157–184.

Melnick, S., & Zeichner, K. (1996). The role of community-based field experiences in preparing teachers for cultural diversity. In K. Zeichner, S. Melnick, & M. Gomez (Eds.), *Currents of reform in preservice teacher education.* (pp. 176–196). New York: Teachers College Press.

National Center for Education Statistics. (2003). Status and trends in the education of Hispanics (Publication No: NCES 2003–008). Retrieved from http://nces. ed.gov/pubs2003/hispanics/SectioT1]& ·

National Center for Education Statistics. (2009). Number and percentage distribution of 3- to 21-year olds served under the Individuals with Disabilities Education Act (IDEA), Part B, and number served as a percentage of total public school enrollment, by type of disability: Selected school years, 1976–77 through 2007–08. Retrieved from http://nces.ed.gov/progrmps/coe/20 I 0/section!Ltable-cwd-l.asg.\

National Center for Education Statistics. (2007). Status and trends in the education of racial and ethnic minorities. (Publication No: NCES 2007–039). Retrieved from http://nces.ed.gov/pubs2007/minoritytrends/.

National Center for Education Statistics. (2010a). Racial/ethnic enrollment in public schools: Indicator 4. Retrieved from http://nces.ed,gov/grograms/coe/2010/sectionl/indic1ltor04.asg.

National Center for Education Statistics. (2010b). The condition of education 2010. (Publication No: NCES 2010–028). Retrieved from http:I/nces.e(].gov/fast-facts/display.asg?id=96.

Organization for Economic Co-operation and Development (2010). *Educating teachers for diversity: Meeting the challenge.* Paris: Office for Economic Cooperation and Development.

Organization for Economic Co-operation and Development (2006). *International migration outlook.* Paris: Office for Economic Cooperation and Development.

Rothstein, R. (2004). *Class and Schools: Using social, economic and education reform to close the Black–White achievement gap.* New York: The Economic Policy Institute.

Seidl, B., & Friend, G. (2002). The unification of church and state: Working together to prepare teachers for diverse classrooms. *Journal of Teacher Education, 53*(2), 142–152.

Sleeter, C. (1995). White preservice students and multicultural education coursework. In J. Larkin & C. Sleeter (Eds.) *Developing multicultural teacher education curricula.* (pp. 17–29). Albany, NY: SUNY Press.

Sleeter, C. (2008). Preparing White teachers for diverse students. In M. Cochran-Smith, S. Feiman Nemser, J. Mcintyre, & K. Demers (Eds.), *Handbook of research on teacher education(3rd edition): Enduring questions* in *changing contexts.* (pp. 559–582). New York: Routledge, Taylor and Francis.

Villegas, A. M., & Lucas, T. (2001). *Preparing culturally responsive teachers: A coherent approach.* Albany, NY: SUNY Press.

Villegas, A. M., & Lucas, T. (2004). Diversifying the teacher workforce: A retrospective and prospective account. In Smylie, M. & Miretzky, D. (Eds.), *Developing the teacher workforce: The I 03rd yearbook of the national society for the study of education* (pp. 0–104). Chicago: University of Chicago Press.

Villegas, A. M., Clewell, B., Anderson, M., Goertz, M., Joy, F., Bruschi, B., &Irvine, J. (1995). *Teaching for diversity: Models for expanding the supply of minority teachers.* Princeton, NJ: ETS.

Villegas, A. M., & Davis, D. (2008). Preparing teachers of color to confront racial/ethnic disparities in educational outcomes. In M. Cochran-Smith, S. Feiman Nemser, J. Mcintyre, & K. Demers (Eds.). *Handbook of research on teacher education(3rd edition): Enduring questions in changing contexts* (pp. 583–605). New York: Routledge, Taylor and Francis.

Weiner, L. (1993). *Preparing teachers for urban schools, lessons from 30 years of school reform.* New York: Teachers College Press.

Zeichner, K. (1993). *Educating teachers for cultural diversity.* East Lansing, MI: Michigan State University, National Center for Research on Teacher Learning.

CHAPTER 9

AMERICAN SCHOOLS, TODAY AND TOMORROW

Alan H. Schoenfeld
Graduate School of Education, Berkeley, California

'Tis education forms the common mind. Just as the twig is bent, the tree's inclined.
—Alexander Pope, 1734, Epistle to Cobham, 149–50

What a daunting assignment! The editors of this volume, O. L. Davis, Jr. and Marcella L. Kysilka, asked the authors to "offer its readers visions of real prospects for American schools during the next 35–40 years." Now, if I could foresee the future—even just a year or two in advance—I would be able to invest in the stock market and make a killing.

As you might guess, I am not on the Forbes list of the world's richest people. In fact, I confess to never having read an issue of Forbes in my life. So, you should take anything I say about the future with the proverbial ton of salt. But, I have been around for a few years and I really care about schooling and its role in American society. So, for what it's worth, I am about to share some ideas about where we have been, where we are, and where we need to go. Whether we go there or not, time will tell.

Schooling for Tomorrow's America, pages 107–127
Copyright © 2014 by Information Age Publishing
All rights of reproduction in any form reserved.

JUST WHAT ARE SCHOOLS FOR, ANYWAY?

From the very beginnings of organized schooling in the United States, various groups have had very different views of the purposes of schooling. Lisa Rosen (2000), an anthropologist, argues that there have been three "master narratives" (or myths) regarding Education in America,

> ...each of which celebrates a particular set of cultural ideals: education for democratic equality (the story that schools should serve the needs of democracy by promoting equality and providing training for citizenship); education for social efficiency (the story that schools should serve the needs of the social and economic order by training students to occupy different positions in society and the economy); and education for social mobility (the story that schools should serve the needs of individuals by providing the means of gaining advantage in competitions for social mobility)." (Rosen, 2000, p. 4)

The first, education for democratic equality, honors the "melting pot" notion of American society that I learned as a school child: America is in large measure a land of immigrants who, over time, have maintained some of their original ethnic, cultural, and religious identities, but have also become transformed by their immersion in American society, and transformed it in the process. Interestingly, this perspective can coexist comfortably with each of the other two—which are polar opposites.

The idea behind education for social efficiency is that schools exist to perpetuate the social order. We need workers—so, schools should train them. Not necessarily as trade schools, but not with the intention of broadening their horizons either. In the early twentieth century it was common for schools to teach just the four basic operations (addition, subtraction, multiplication, division) in mathematics, and no more. Why? Because store clerks would need to be facile with arithmetic, but they surely would not need more mathematical knowledge than that. Moreover, too much knowledge can make people unhappy with their lot, and potentially dangerous. (The clearest example of this is that before and during the civil war, it was illegal in some states to teach slaves to read.)

In contrast, the idea behind education for social mobility is that of America as the idealized meritocracy: first, "You can grow up to be President," people should rise through American society on the basis of talent and hard work (cf. Horatio Alger); and second, schools should be the mechanism by which people with radically different backgrounds and home advantages are offered the knowledge and skills that will enable them to make the best of themselves.

Let me put my cards on the table. I am an idealist who draws strongly upon the traditions of education for democratic equality and education for social mobility. I think that the right kind of education is, and should be, liberating and empowering, and that everybody should have access to it. From my perspective, education should give everyone the tools by which to "make it" in American society; moreover, if it's done right, the people who emerge from the right kinds of schooling will be best positioned to contribute to a vibrant and powerful American society.

So, what do I mean by the right kind of education? For me, the main goal of education is to produce inquisitive, powerful and productive, and highly moral, thinkers and doers! Knowledge in the form of facts, skills, and conceptual understandings is important; but it is not enough. In addition, powerful thinkers have certain intellectual habits of mind: inquisitiveness, a wish to understand, and a predilection to think things through so that their arguments are grounded in knowledge and reason. This is the case no matter what the discipline. Different subject areas provide different tools, but within any discipline one can be taught to "master" content passively or to live and breathe the spirit of the discipline.

I am all for the latter. I am a reader (newspapers, books, you name it) because I love finding out about things. Newspapers tell me about current events; the most prominent ones as I write this essay being the massive social upheavals in Egypt and surrounding nations. But one needs a context. Why are things happening now, and how did today's events get shaped by the recent and not-so-recent past? That's where history comes in: the unrest in Egypt becomes more understandable when one sees how Mubarak's rule became increasingly oppressive over 30 years, how social media made it possible for the democratic opposition to organize; and more. I learned in today's New York Times (Stolberg, 2011, page 1) that an 83-year old scholar named Gene Sharp has written a series of "practical writings on nonviolent revolution— most notably, *From Dictatorship to Democracy*, a 93-page guide to toppling autocrats, available for download in 24 languages—that have inspired dissidents around the world, including in Burma, Bosnia, Estonia and Zimbabwe, and now Tunisia and Egypt." (The article goes on to explain Sharp's idea that violent rebellion plays to the strengths of autocrats, and points to a series of nonviolent protest methods). Seeing how all these pieces of the puzzle fit together is truly exciting.[1]

Purely as a matter of coincidence—the novel had been on my "waiting to be read" shelf for close to a year, and I started it shortly before the unrest in Egypt—I happened to read Alaa Al Aswamy's novel *The Yacoubian Building*. I bought it because a friend recommended it as a rich and engaging story (which it is); as a bonus, I got what the New Review of Books, in the blurb on the book's cover, calls "an amazing glimpse of modern Egyptian society and culture." That provided yet another, and completely unexpected, perspective on current events. But, I did not read the book for that; I read it for fun—for the story, the characters, flow of language. I get a visceral pleasure when a book is well written. I certainly did not read it looking for pragmatic information (I do plenty of that in my day job!), or to decode language, or to get more facts in my personal knowledge base. The same is true of other books I have read recently, from Muriel Barbery's, *The Elegance of the Hedgehog* (2006) to Jerome Groopman's edited collection, *The Best American Science Writing* (2010)—in which I was stimulated to think about the ethics of organ donations, the question of whether humans are evolving more rapidly than previously thought, and more. What fun! There's a bumper sticker that says "If you can read, thank a teacher." Even more, if you love to read, think how much you owe to the ones who taught you!

Having referred in passing to the sciences, let me say a bit more—because mathematics and the sciences can either be experienced as disciplines in which you're beaten over the head with facts, or as disciplines in which we get to see how things work. Do you remember the quadratic formula? I do; but that's because I'm a "math guy" and I know how and why it works. For most people, learning it was an act of rote memorization, and the memory trace is long gone. That's a real shame. Approached in the right way—from pre-school through graduate school—mathematics is an amazing subject in which things fit together almost magically. But, the difference between mathematics and magic is that in math you can figure out why things work the way they do. Here is a simple observation made by many young school children: when they add two odd whole numbers, the result is an even number. Now, that can give rise to some deep questions: Will this always happen? How could you know, since the odd numbers go on forever"? It may surprise you to know that third graders can grapple, successfully, with such questions (Ball & Bass, 2000; Schoenfeld, 2008a; Stylianides, 2005). And when they generate those questions and get to pursue them, they are that much more engaged. At a somewhat more advanced level, here is a problem you can approach in various ways: Take any three digit number and write it down twice to make a six digit number. For example, the number 246 produces the 6-digit number 246,246. I bet you a dollar that your six digit number can be divided by 7 without leaving a remainder. OK, I was lucky. I bet you five dollars that the quotient from the previous division can be divided by 11 without leaving a remainder. So, I got lucky again. I bet you 25 dollars that the quotient from the previous division can be divided by 13 without leaving a remainder. You don't have to pay me if you can explain why.

Discussions of this problem get students engaged; and in the course of the discussions, the students learn a lot of mathematics. In fact, I would argue that a very large percentage of the mathematics that we teach as coming "from above" can instead be developed as a set of reasonable answers to some very reasonable questions. If you look at mathematical issues in the right ways, then math makes sense—so, the question is how kids can learn mathematics as an act of sense-making. Much the same is the case for science, which can either be treated as a discipline in which the students' job is to master facts, concepts, and procedures, or as a form of inquiry in which we make observations, note interesting relation-ships, and try to figure out what makes them work the ways they do.

What I want is for our classrooms and schools to produce people who have these habits of mind—people who are intellectually curious, who ask ques-tions, and who are equipped both by disposition and by the disciplinary tools they have learned, to grapple with those questions. This, I believe, is the best way to equip today's youth for tomorrow's America. It's best for them as indi-viduals: people with the attributes I have described are both resourceful (with knowledge one of their resources) and flexible. And, if there is one thing that we know about the future, it's that things will be changing at astonishing speed. Those who only have a body of skills will soon find themselves outpaced. Those who are resourceful and flexible will be able to learn what they need to know as the world changes. I also believe that this is what is best for American society as a whole: as I see it, a tradition of flexibility and resourcefulness through the centuries is a large part of what has made us the nation we are. Finally, I believe that as a matter of social justice, everyone should have access to the kinds of schooling that will produce curious, knowledgeable, and productive learners.

WHAT SHOULD CLASSROOMS LOOK LIKE?

What kinds of classroom environments will produce kids who are knowl-edgeable, independent thinkers? Here the research has a lot to say. One valuable reference is the National Research Council's 2002 volume, *How People Learn*. The authors of that volume argue compellingly that produc-tive learning environments have the following properties:

1. They are learner-centered, meaning that they "pay careful attention to the knowledge, skills, attitudes, and beliefs that learners bring to the educational setting" (p. 133.) "Accomplished teachers ... respect and understand learners' prior experiences and understandings, assuming that these can serve as a foundation on which to build bridges to new understandings" (p. 136).
2. They are knowledge-centered, meaning that significant thought has gone into conceptualizing the content to be learned in ways that important ideas are highlighted, and that knowledge and skills are acquired in ways that support planning, strategic thinking, and trans-fer. They should also foster principled and coherent reasoning and explanation, self-monitoring, and reflection (pp. 136–139).
3. They are assessment-centered, but in particular ways: the focus is not on testing at the end of instruction to demonstrate what students know and can do (although that is important, of course), but rather on the idea of formative assessment—providing students with ongo-

ing feedback and opportunities for revision that are consistent with learning goals (including planning strategic thinking, and transfer) (pp. 139–144).

4. They are community-centered: "At the level of classrooms and schools, learning seems to be enhanced by social norms that value the search for understanding and allow students (and teachers) the freedom to make mistakes in order to learn" (p. 145).

That is somewhat abstract, so let me give another framing, which focuses more on the students themselves and how they experience the learning. This is the "productive disciplinary engagement" framework developed by Randi Engle and colleagues (Engle, 2011; Engle & Conant, 2002). Engle has conducted intensive reviews of the best known international examples of highly productive learning environments—classrooms or programs that are known for producing the kinds of knowledgeable and inquisitive thinkers described above. The dimensions of such environments are highlighted in what follows.

PROBLEMATIZING

Learning is not simply about ingesting information; it is about developing powerful habits of mind, of learning to figure out "what counts" and how to pursue relevant theoretical and practical issues in a disciplined way. For example, Engle and Conant describe an ongoing classroom discussion regarding orcas, commonly known as "killer whales." The class, which had been studying whales, had gone to Marine World on a field trip. They were told by a trainer that orcas are not whales, but members of the dolphin family. This resulted in a "big ol' argument" when the students returned to school—a discussion in which the students "did their homework" by looking up resources and, over time, sorting out conflicting opinions in those sources.

In the third grade mathematics class I mentioned above, as the students pursued the question of whether the sum of two odd number had to be even, they came to realize that each odd number consists of a number of pairs with one left over; when you add the two odd numbers, the two "leftover" singletons can be made into a pair, so the sum is made up of pairs—and is thus even (Ball & Bass, 2000; Schoenfeld, 2008a; Stylianides, 2005).

Sometimes, a simple shift in framing can make a big difference. Most math classes, for example, give students exercises phrased in the form "Show that (some particular thing) is true." John Mason (personal communication) says that classroom discussions shift dramatically when the exercise is phrased as "My friend says (some particular thing) is true. Is she right? If she is, show why. If she isn't, give an example that demonstrates she's wrong." More generally, asking "Do we think that's the case? If so, why?" in response to almost any assertion—be it about the character traits of a novel's protagonist, the causes of the Civil war, one's reaction to a work of art, or a mathematical or scientific claim—opens issues up for discussion and lets it be known that asking such questions is a good thing to do.

AGENCY AND AUTHORITY

Powerful learners are active, not passive. Problematizing—asking good questions and not taking things at face value—is a start. But then, one needs the wherewithal to follow up in the right ways. That's what personal agency is all about. People with a sense of agency feel entitled to pursue the issues they raise. Good learning environments help students develop that sense of agency, by helping students to pursue and refine their ideas. There's no better reward for thinking hard than to gain clear ownership of an idea!

There are multiple meanings to the word "authority," so let me be sure to emphasize the right one here. What I don't mean is the kind of autocratic authority that shuts conversations down. That can be a serious problem, whether the authority is wielded by a teacher or a student. The authority Engle and colleagues talk about ("she's an authority in the field") is rooted in the notion of authorship—that one authors (is the source of) ideas, and that as one's ideas take hold, one gains credibility and is listened to. Of course, when people listen to you, you are likely to have a strong sense of agency.

ACCOUNTABILITY

Not all ideas or opinions are created equal. Is shouting louder a form of authority? Not in the right classrooms, and that's where accountability comes in.

There is accountability to the subject matter, both in terms of subject matter knowledge and the patterns of reasoning that are appropriate for the discipline. A well crafted argument depends on disciplinary knowledge. You cannot argue about the causes of the civil war unless you have some facts at your disposal; you cannot write a compelling essay unless you know how to make a thesis statement and marshal your arguments in support of it; and you cannot claim something in mathematics is true because "I tried a whole lot of examples and it always worked." In a science class, you play by the rules of science. So, a large part of learning consists of learning the rules of the game in each subject area, and getting good at working within those rules. (To return to an earlier example: the third graders who argued that the sum of two odd whole numbers must be even actually produced a proof that any university mathematician would accept as valid.)

There is also accountability to the classroom community—to the teacher and to other students. One of my favorite classroom videotapes shows a group of students working together. The teacher comes by and asks the group if they are ready to discuss their work. The students say yes, and the teacher asks one student to explain her/their reasoning. As the teacher probes her reasoning (accountability to the discipline—the teacher was not satisfied with "just" the correct answer, but pushed for deep understanding), the student gets confused. Without any negative affect the teacher says that she will return when the student is ready to continue. After the teacher moves away, another student says to the one who'd gotten confused, "When she comes back, just tell her this...." The first student's response to this was, in essence, "Now look. I don't understand what you just said, even though I can repeat it. You know the teacher is going to ask me questions to find out if I really understand it, and I won't be able to answer her. Since you understand this, your job is to make sure I do." The two students then work together. When the teacher comes back, the first student demonstrates solid understanding. (And, her happiness with the understanding she has demonstrated is evident. When accountability works right, agency and authority are increased.)

RESOURCES

A one-liner suffices here: highly productive learning environments need to include sufficient resources to support the intellectual activities described above. And this raises some new issues. See the next section.

WHAT ABOUT TECHNOLOGY?

Up to this point, my argument has been "timeless." The attributes of powerful learners and powerful learning environments described in the previous two sections were true when KDP was founded a century ago, and will be true when KDP celebrates its bicentennial. But the world has changed dramatically—even if most classrooms have not. And, available technologies are changing the nature of what it means to make good use of information.

Let me begin by describing the way my research group works. In one of my projects, we are looking at the impact that different styles of teaching have on student learning in algebra. To do that, we need to build (or borrow) some tools—classroom observation schemes, assessments of algebraic understanding, and more. For the most part we use the web to track many of these down. We started by emailing drafts to each other, but then things got complicated. In meetings, we would all be looking at the same document and suggesting/making changes, so we used Google Docs in order to work on documents simultaneously. But, keeping track of previous versions (sometimes we want to return to a previous version) and organizing them became an individual challenge, so we started using Dropbox to organize both our history and current versions. When I log on, the newest versions of our documents are there waiting for me.

In our meetings, there are times when everyone's working with a laptop as we talk. This may seem antisocial, but there is plenty of eye contact, and the laptops are either used for changing collective documents (in which case we were all focusing on the same things) or for looking up information. A question will come up, and people will start looking for information on the web. It is trite by now, but we all have libraries at our fingertips (literally, in that we can access our university's library holdings electronically).

But, with universal access to knowledge comes new problems. Guess what? You should not believe everything you read! Instead of living in a classroom where there might be one or a few "authoritative" texts, we have access to a huge range of information, which may or may not be reliable. So, an important part of our "literacy" consists of our being able to sift through conflicting information, to evaluate its credibility. (An informational note: you can sort through the "orca: whale or dolphin" debate in relatively short order today, using the web. But being able to find information is not the key: it is being able to evaluate that information. There's Wikipedia, there's Answers.com, and there's Dr. Galapagos; there's Marinebio.org, National Geographic, Answerbag, and, oh yes, there's the American Cetacean Society.)

In short, my students and I depend on the technology for a huge part of what we do, both in finding information and in providing tools for managing it. We use somewhat different techniques, with a greater emphasis on judging the quality of available information (which is plentiful) than on merely amassing it. Such are the skills we are using today—and which very few classrooms in the world are using today. The fact that information technologies have made few inroads into our classrooms is a problem, and it will be more of a problem as we move further into the twenty-first century. Before or after school, many of our students are expert web-users; but when they enter the classroom they enter a world that is a generation or two behind them, and that is not preparing them for the world they live in much less for the future. In some classrooms I have visited, the only technology I have seen is when students use their cell phones to text each other when they think the teacher is not looking.

Now, I should be clear about this: I am neither technophile nor technophobe. I use technology, but I have never been a fan of the "latest and greatest." I use it when I have been convinced that what I want to do will be easier using the technology, even considering the cost of learning to use it.

In the world outside of schools, technology is a fact of life; in the years to come, that will be so much more the case. On the one hand, to fail to use it wisely, and to fail to help our students to use it wisely, is an abdication of moral and intellectual responsibility. On the other hand, it should not be used faddishly. The solution is to use it in ways that matter. To return to the themes of the previous two sections: if students are working on meaningful problems; if they have opportunities to develop agency and authority as they do so; if they are helped to pick up disciplinary knowledge and to use the reasoning practices of the disciplines; if they do so in ways that contribute to their learning communities; and if they have access to the resources they need, including the technological resources to which they will have access outside of school and in the workplace, then we will be preparing students for whatever challenges they face when they graduate.

If it is still up on the web when you read this article, you might want to look at the video entitled "did you know" at http://www.youtube.com/watch?v=cL9Wu2kWwSY. The music is a little portentous, but some of the numbers are pretty amazing. For example, that "the U.S. department of labor estimates that today's learner will have 10–14 jobs by the age of 38." We had better be preparing people to be flexible thinkers! And, to return to my comments in the first section: the revolutionary changes in Egyptian and neighboring societies over recent weeks and months were stimulated and abetted by social media. We can harness and adapt them, and have students make intelligent, collaborative progress on interesting problems (e.g., the knowledge forum: Bereiter & Scardamalia, 2003). Or, we can continue to ignore technologies—at our peril.

DEMOGRAPHICS

The American body politic is evolving, and it will continue to evolve. California, which leads the nation in demographic trends, reached a watershed in late 2010. The headline from the November 13, 2010 San Francisco Chronicle (Kane, 2010) relays the news: "Latino kids now majority in state's public schools." Here are the data.

> Latinos now make up a majority of California's public school students, cracking the 50% barrier for the first time in the state's history," according to data released Friday by the state Department of Education.

> Almost 50.4% of the state's students in the 2009–2010 school year identified themselves as Hispanic or Latino, up 1.36% from the previous year. In comparison, 27% of California's 6.2 million students identified themselves

as White, 9% as Asian and 7% as Black. Students calling themselves Filipino, Pacific Islander, Native American or other total almost 7%.

That is: 73% of California's public school students self-identify as non White. The challenge is, how will we serve these students adequately? In simplest terms, the most powerful instruction respects and builds upon the knowledge that students bring with them, helping to develop agency and authority.

There is research in various subject areas suggesting how this can be done. For example, Luis Moll and colleagues (Gonzalez, Andrade, Civil, & Moll, 2001; Moll, Amanti, Neff, & Gonzalez, 1992; Moll & Gonzalez, 2004) discuss the "funds of knowledge" that students bring with them—knowledge upon which school knowledge can be built and expanded. This is a very different view of students than the "deficit" view, in which students who don't have the expected cultural and school backgrounds are labeled as being in need of remediation. Carol Lee's work on literacy exemplifies this kind of approach; she builds on what students know and care about, introducing them to sophisticated textual analyses (Lee, 1995; see also Gutierrez & Rogoff, 2003).

A related idea is that culturally responsive pedagogy (Ladson-Billings, 1994, 1995) can create classroom communities that are responsive to students and can help them feel empowered to learn. A lovely example in science teaching is the Cheche Konnen project (Rosebery, Warren, & Conant, 1992; Rosebery, Warren, Ogonowski & Ballenger, 2005; Warren & Rosebery, 1995). Cheche Konnen emphasizes the sensemaking resources those children from ethnically and linguistically diverse backgrounds bring to the study of science. The articles referenced here show how instruction can build on them.

OUTSIDE FACTORS, PART I:
PRESSURES AND OPPORTUNITIES

The "standards movement" has transformed the landscape of American education, and not all for the good. The original motivation, as embodied by the first set of national standards, the national Council of Teachers of Mathematics' (1989) Curriculum and Evaluation Standards for School Mathematics, was very simple: As a nation, we needed some clarity on the "big ideas" in the mathematics curriculum. The original Standards were aspirational: in essence they said, "These are the kinds of things we would like students to know." Given the incoherence of our national system—fifty states, each with its own set of standards—the idea of national consensus on important curricular goals was (to some, at least) a welcome idea, not just in mathematics, but in all content areas.

But then the "standards movement" took on a life of its own—and it took a serious turn for the worse with the enactment of the No Child Left Behind Act of 2001. NCLB, as it is known, institutionalized standards as "must knows;" and it institutionalized testing to make sure kids knew what they were supposed to. Each state had to establish its own standards, and to test for them. The system had few incentives for improvement but lots of penalties for failing to meet the standards. Not surprisingly, there was an increased emphasis on testing, and preparing for the (often not very good, but very high stakes) tests. With 50 different sets of standards, we had nationally institutionalized incoherence.

As I write, the move toward Common Core State Standards provides a promising but dangerous opportunity. Any set of standards can be good or bad, and with high stakes assessments as part of an accountability system, the standards-plus-assessments system can drive the educational system in either good or bad ways. We have seen that over the past decade, with some states introducing standards that are focused on skills and procedures, while other states have demanded conceptual understanding and problem solving. But now, with more than 80% of the states signing on to the Common Core State Standards, we have the potential for significant, nationwide improvement—or a significant nationwide intellectual disaster. This will all depend on how the Common Core State Standards are interpreted, especially with regard to assessment.

The Standards themselves, in English Language Arts and in Mathematics, are quite reasonable. This may sound like damning with faint praise—and I do have my quibbles, of course—but the fact that they are solid documents is in fact a substantial achievement, given the fact that they were produced in a matter of months. (By way of comparison, a national team of two dozen people took three years, including a very substantial feedback and revision process, to produce NCTM's (2000) Principles and Standards for School Mathematics.) The Common Core State Standards for English Language Arts & Literacy In History/Social Studies, Science, and Technical Subjects (CCSSI-ELA, 2010a) presents a "portrait" of what it means for students to be(come) literate individuals:

- They demonstrate independence.
- They build strong content knowledge.
- They respond to the varying demands of audience, task, purpose, and discipline.
- They comprehend as well as critique.
- They value evidence.
- They use technology and digital media strategically and capably.
- They come to understand other perspectives and cultures (p. 7).

I can see myself in this description; it resonates reasonably well with the portrait of me as a reader that began this essay.

The common core standards for mathematics (CCSI-M, 2010b), rather than merely listing the content that students should master,[2] list as well a set of desirable mathematical practices—that is, ways of acting mathematically. According to CCSI-M, people who are mathematically proficient

- make sense of problems and persevere in solving them,
- reason abstractly and quantitatively,
- construct viable arguments and critique the reasoning of others,
- model with mathematics,
- use appropriate tools strategically,
- attend to precision,
- look for and make use of structure, and
- look for and express regularity in repeated reasoning.

These are pretty reasonable mathematical habits of mind; I think I see myself in them too. Having in mind the discussion of productive classroom environments earlier in this chapter, I note that one might look for a bit more problematizing, and so forth; but I think if our students demonstrated the capacities in the sets of bullets taken from the Common Core State Standards, they would be pretty well prepared.

Will they be well prepared by our system? It depends. First, it depends on curricula. Teaching for the kinds of rich understanding we hope to develop, in all fields, requires effective support materials. Over the past decades some of our curricular materials have gotten much better, and the students who have learned from them have done better—but given the uneven patchwork of standards across the nation, and the comparably uneven curricula that are implemented nationwide, real progress has been negligible. We have a long way to go, and it will take a concerted effort.

One thing we have learned in mathematics, both nationally and internationally is that solidly build standards-based curricula can make a significant difference. (Schoenfeld, 2004, 2008b; Senk, 2003; Tomer, Schoenfeld, & Reiss, 2008). However, what gets published is, to put it bluntly, usually a commercial rather than an intellectual decision. After the NCTM Standards were published in 1989, publishers made it clear that they were not about to publish standards-based materials, because they represented a huge financial risk. I was one of the authors of the 1992 California mathematics Framework. The most consistent attendees at our open public meetings were publishers' representatives. They made it absolutely clear that, given the cost of producing a K–8 textbook series in mathematics, they were not about to invest in an unproven concept such as standards-based texts. The reason such texts did get produced was that the National

Science Foundation issued a request for proposals for groups to produce standards-based curricula—and those curricula did make their way into the marketplace, and when they proved viable, they were picked up by commercial publishers. Of course, now, with more than 80% of the states signed on to the common core standards process, there are obvious incentives for the big publishers to produce texts that appear aligned with the Common Core State Standards. But, the textbook production and selection processes are commercially driven and highly political; it is not at all clear just what kinds of materials will prevail in the market. And as we all know, the materials one teaches with make a big difference.

But even more important than the curricula are the assessments. Some years ago my friend and colleague Hugh Burkhardt coined the acronym WYTIWYG—"What You Test Is What You Get." All of us who live in classrooms know it's a reality. Never mind your noble goals: the month or two before the high stakes tests, 90% of the classrooms around the country are focused on drilling for the tests. When those tests are multiple choice tests of basic skills, it is a waste and a perversion of class time. I could provide lots of evidence about how drilling for such tests provide ephemeral gains—student knowledge is fragile and soon forgotten—but I assume I would be preaching to the choir. You all know what a waste of time prepping students for dinky high stakes tests really is. For a thoughtful discussion of the role of high stakes testing in supporting the implementation of standards, see Black, Burkhardt, Daro, Jones, Lappan, Pead, & Stephens, 2011.[3]

To put things simply, the nature of the high stakes tests that will be used to assess students' proficiency on the CCSS is a BIG deal. There are many ways to build assessments that really focus on the aspects of literacy and mathematical skills bulleted above. Properly used, high quality formative and summative assessments can drive the system in very positive directions. But the potential for abuse is significant, especially if the people building the state-wide assessment systems decide to "cheap out" by using poorly designed technological "solutions" to the testing "problem."

Here is a story of how that can happen. Approximately 20 years ago I was approached by ETS and asked if I would be willing to serve on the committee that wrote the Advanced Mathematics examination for the Graduate Record Exam (GRE). I remembered the exam as being one of the worst testing experiences of my life—three hours of high pressure hell, in which I had to race through about 60 multiple choice problems that rewarded cleverness rather than deep mathematical thinking. So, I asked if I could see a copy of the current exam. After doing so, I told the committee liaison, "This feels almost identical to the GRE advanced mathematics exam I took 25 years ago. I hated it then, and I hate it now. I will join the committee only if there is a chance we can change it." I was told there was a chance that we could (ETS knew that the test correlated well with first year grades in graduate school, but not with much else, so an improved exam would be a good thing), and I joined the committee. Some other like-minded people joined the committee, and we began to pilot what we thought was a meaningful exam. We spent about five years building an essay test focusing on mathematical reasoning and argumentation, the skills that graduate students really need. And, we were in the middle of pilot-testing that essay test, when . . .

ETS decided that its future lay in computer-adaptive testing. There are virtues to computer-adaptive testing, of course: the grading process is cheap and efficient, and students find out how well they did right after finishing the test. The way scoring works is that the exam starts with a problem of medium difficulty. If the student gets it right, then the next problem is harder and the student's potential GRE score goes up. If the student gets it wrong, then the next problem is easier and the student's potential GRE score goes down. In less time than it took for the old written multiple choice test, the student finishes the exam and walks out with a score. *But* . . . the problems used for the test are the old ones, because (a) they had to be answered fast and (b) those were the ones ETS had the statistics for. In other words, the move to computer-adaptive testing depended on using, the old, horrid multiple-choice problems—and it destroyed the attempt to implement, instead, a test that actually focused on the skills we wanted to see. You can guess which system is still in use, 20 years later.

Now, I know that we are promised technological wonders to support new assessments–technologies that can read and assess student essays, and so forth. To be sure, we have seen astounding advances in technologies over the past decade(s). It might be possible to use technology wisely to build truly spectacular assessment systems, that help students and teachers understand students' progress toward the standards. But decisions on how to implement assessments will be made very soon, and whatever assessments are chosen will have to be ready for use very fast—so there is a serious chance of history repeating itself, this time on a larger scale. Whether or not it does will depend on whether and how we raise our voices, and whether and how they are heard.

This brings me to my final section, on teaching as a profession.

OUTSIDE/INSIDE FACTORS, PART 2

The Need to Become More of a "Learning Profession"

Let me start by stating what you know, but so few people understand. Teaching is an extraordinarily challenging profession; it demands a huge amount of work, typically in return for little respect and low pay. The vast majority of teachers are hard working. They were attracted to the field, and stay in it, because of a love of children and subject matter, and the intrinsic gratification of helping students learn.

At the same time, there are a host of issues that we have not confronted as a profession and that we need to. To put things bluntly, I think the profession of teaching is at stake. Either we will move collectively to bolster teaching as a true profession, in which case the schools of tomorrow will be much more exciting places to teach than they are currently, or we will not, in which case teaching is likely to be increasingly de-skilled and tomorrow's schools will be increasingly depressing places for students and teachers alike.

Most people simply do not understand effective teaching. According to folk wisdom, the good teacher is the one who has half a dozen coherent explanations in his or her back pocket. The assumption is that if the first one does not sink in, maybe the second will; if the second does not, maybe the third one will; and so on. This view is predicated on the "blank slate" or "empty jug" notion of students and knowledge: The students are seen as waiting for knowledge to be "written on" or "poured into" them. Wrong, wrong, wrong: We know full well that students actively construct knowledge, sometimes correctly and sometimes incorrectly; and that if they have an incorrect version of some concept, repeating the correct version is not likely to be effective. They have heard the explanations; they have (mis)understood them; and saying the same thing over again is not likely to change their misunderstandings. Thus, being an effective teacher means anticipating students' understandings and misunderstandings, being able to identify them (that is why formative assessment is such a big deal), and having in one's back pocket a number of resources that enable one to "meet the students where they are" and move them forward. It is about being receptive to student thinking, and working with it in productive ways.

It is odd that most people do not get this. We know that if people learning music develop bad habits, it is really hard to unlearn those habits—and if those habits are not unlearned, then the aspiring musician will not progress very far. We know that sport coaches work very closely with their charges to identity productive and unproductive behaviors, and shape them very carefully. So "diagnosis" or "formative assessment" is a big part of the game. But people do not think this way when it comes to teaching. The simple view that most people have is, "if you know your subject matter and you can explain things clearly, you are set." That view is not only wrong, it is dangerous (e.g., Darling-Hammond & Bransford, 2005).

Those assumptions frame our national approach to teaching as a profession, and they are a big problem. They allow us to believe (at least structurally) that a year of training can prepare someone to run a classroom. Thus "prepared," most teachers are dumped into their own classrooms, with few external resources or opportunities to learn. Dan Lortie (1977) referred to the "egg crate" culture of schools: imagine a school as an egg carton, with each compartment pretty much isolated and insulated from the others. How, in this kind of organization, given a full work day and then plenty to do at night, is a teacher to learn except slowly and painfully, from his or her own experience?

It does not have to be this way. The Japanese, for example, believe that no matter how talented a beginning teacher might be, it takes a decade, with the support of one's colleagues, for that teacher to develop into an expert teacher. As a result, the Japanese arrange teachers' work weeks differently than we do: most schools have common work spaces for teachers and common work/planning times. In the elementary schools, where "lesson study" is a mainstream practice, teachers collaborate on the design and teaching of lessons—a mechanism from which beginning teachers can learn continually from those who are more experienced. That is, learning time is officially defined as part of the work week. In such circumstances, teachers have the opportunity and support to develop the kinds of skills and understandings that enable them to become increasingly proficient.[4]

What we have seen in the United States over the past decade or more has been a program aimed at the de-skilling of teachers, rather than an acknowledgment of the complexities of teaching. That is what low-level standardized tests, high stakes accountability, pacing plans with assessments every two weeks, and such, are all about. The question is, will we take the steps that are necessary to increase our own professionalism, and in the process, reassert what it means to be real teachers? Doing so will involve a combination of very difficult things. It will involve a public relations campaign, to inform people of just what a challenge it is to teach well, and why. It will involve lobbying to arrange our work weeks so that we have the opportunities to interact professionally on the job.[5] It will also involve more transparency—letting others into our classrooms as we work together to improve, and sharing our successes and failures. Finally, it will involve developing meaningful standards for the profession, and upholding them. This may be scary, but the alternative is far scarier. Others, who do not necessarily understand what teaching is all about, are defining such standards de facto by using student scores on standardized tests to rate teacher quality. The question is, will we stand up for what is right in terms of teaching, and serving our students, or let others define what effective teaching means?

Not to be melodramatic, but the future of American schooling hangs in the balance.

SOME FINAL WORDS

I did not know whether to start this last section with the phrase "I am an optimist at heart" or "I am a teacher at heart." I am both, of course. I aspire to the vision of classrooms described in the section "what should classrooms look like?" I also think that, despite the challenges described in the preceding two sections of this paper, we have made tremendous strides toward that vision. We know so much more about thinking, teaching, and learning than when I began doing research. Much of that understanding has been translated into practical terms: the original "standards movement" was grounded in the basic research of the 1970s and 1980s, and we now have models of effective standards-based instruction that are supported by widely used standards-based texts. This is a solid base to build on, toward the even more ambitious vision described in this paper. Will we get there? It depends on many factors, some of which may not be in our control. But we owe it to our current and future students (and to ourselves) to give it our best shot.

NOTES

1. I should note that I was bored by my history classes as a student. I was one of legions of students who memorized the fact that the battle of Hastings was fought in 1066, and so on—but those facts had no "life" for me. The challenge is to make our disciplines come alive for our students.

2. The quite reasonable concept behind content selection on the CCSS-M is that the main goal should be focus and coherence rather than scattershot coverage. Getting one's head around a reasonable number of big ideas is, as an organizing principle, much preferable to trying to ingest a host of smaller and less integrated concepts.

3. I do note that the kind of testing mania we have in the United States is not universal. Various nations in Europe and Scandinavia (which score quite well on TIMSS and PISA) manage to do so without such an emphasis on testing.

4. For a discussion of the educational system in Japan, including a discussion of teacher professionalism, see National Institute on Student Achievement, Curriculum, and Assessment, 1998; for a discussion of lesson study, see Fernandez & Yoshida, 2004; for a discussion of possible trajectories of teacher professionalism in the United States, see Schoenfeld, 2010.

5. An example: in Berkeley, the Diversity in Mathematics Education project began with a volunteer seminar after school. One of the things that happened in the seminar was that teachers at different schools through the district finally had the opportunity to compare notes, and then work together. This experience was so powerful that the following year the teachers' union negotiated a different work schedule. School days were lengthened on Monday, Tuesday, Thursday, and Friday, so that school could end earlier on Wednesdays and teachers could get together on a regular basis, "on the clock," for professional development. Thus, professional development became part of the job (see Schoenfeld, 2009).

REFERENCES

Al Aswany, A. (2004). *The Yacoubian building.* New York: Harper Perennial.

Ball, D. L., & Bass, H. (2000). Making believe: The collective construction of public mathematical knowledge in the elementary classroom. In D. C. Phillips (Ed.), *Yearbook of the national society for the study of education, constructivism in education* (pp. 193–224). Chicago: University of Chicago Press.

Barbery, M. (2006) *The elegance of the hedgehog.* New York: Europa.

Bereiter, C., & Scardamalia, M. (2003). Learning to work creatively with knowledge. In E. De Corte, L. Verschaffel, N. Entwistle, & J. van Merrienboer (Eds.), *Powerful learning environments: Unraveling basic components and dimensions* (pp. 55–68). (Advances in Learning and Instruction Series). Oxford, UK: Elsevier Science.

Black, P. Burkhardt, H., Daro, P., Jones, L., Lappan, G., Pead, & Stephens, M. (2011). *High-stakes examinations to support policy: Design, development and implementation.* (White papers produced by the Working Group on Examinations and Policy of the International Society for Design and Development in Education for the two national assessment consortia can be downloaded from http://www.mathshell.org/papers/pdf/ISDDE_PARCC_Feb11.pdf and http://www.mathshell.org/papers/pdf/ISDDE_SBAC_Feb11.pdf.)

Common Core Standards Initiative. (2010a). *Common core state standards for English language arts & literacy in history/social studies, science, and technical subjects.* Can be downloaded from http://www.corestandards.org/the-standards

Common Core Standards Initiative. (2010b). *Common core state standards for Mathematics.* Can be downloaded from http://www.corestandards.org/the-standards

Darling-Hammond, L., & Bransford, J. (Eds.). (2005). *Preparing teachers for a changing world.* San Francisco: Jossey-Bass.

Engle, R. A. (2011). The productive disciplinary engagement framework: Origins, key concepts, and continuing developments. In D. Y. Dai (Ed.), *Design research on learning and thinking in educational settings: Enhancing intellectual growth and functioning* (pp. 161–200). London: Taylor & Francis.

Engle, R. A., & Conant, F. R. (2002). Guiding principles for fostering productive disciplinary engagement: Explaining an emergent argument in a community of learners classroom. *Cognition and Instruction, 20*(4), 399–483.

Fernandez, C., & Yoshida, M. (2004). Lesson study: A Japanese approach to improving mathematics teaching and learning. Mahwah, NJ: Erlbaum.

Gonzalez, N., Andrade, R., Civil, M., & Moll, L. (2001). Bridging funds of distributed knowledge: Creating zones of practices in mathematics. *Journal of Education for Students Placed at Risk, 6*(1–2), 115–132.

Groopman, J. (2010). *The best American science writing 2010.* New York: Harper Collins.

Gutierrez, K., & Rogoff, B. (2003). Cultural ways of learning: Individual traits or repertoires of practice. *Educational Researcher 32*(5), 19–25.

Kane, W. (2010, November 13). Latino kids now majority in state's public schools. *San Francisco Chronicle.* Downloaded February 19, 2011 from http://articles.sfgate.com/2010-11-13/news/24830132_1_latino-parents-latino-voters lisa-garcia-bed

Ladson-Billings, G. (1994). *The dreamkeepers.* San Francisco: Jossey-Bass.

Ladson-Billings, G. (1995). But that's just good teaching! The case for culturally relevant pedagogy. *Theory into Practice, 34*(3), 159–165.

Lee, C. D. (1995). Signifying as a scaffold for literary interpretation. *Journal of Black Psychology, 21*(4), 357–381.

Lortie, S. (1977). *Schoolteacher: A sociological study.* Chicago: University of Chicago press.

Moll, L. C., Amanti, C., Neff, D., & Gonzalez, N. (1992). Funds of knowledge for teaching: Using a qualitative approach to connect homes and classrooms. *Theory Into Practice, 31*(2), 132–141.

Moll, L., & Gonzalez, N. (2004). Engaging life: A funds-of-knowledge approach to multicultural education. In J. Banks & C. Banks (Eds.), *Handbook of research on multicultural education* (pp. 699–715). San Francisco: Jossey-Bass.

National Institute on Student Achievement, Curriculum, and Assessment. (1998). *The educational system in Japan: Case study findings.* Washington, DC: U.S. Department of Education, Office of Educational Research and Improvement.

National Research Council (2002). How people learn (Expanded Edition). Washington DC: National Academy Press.

National Council of Teachers of Mathematics. (1989). *Curriculum and evaluation standards for school mathematics.* Reston, VA: NCTM.

National Council of Teachers of Mathematics. (2000). *Principles and Standards for School Mathematics.* Reston, VA: NCTM.

Rosebery, A., Warren, B., & Conant, F. (1992). Appropriating scientific discourse: Findings from language minority classrooms. *Journal of the Learning Sciences, 2,* 61–94.

Rosebery, A., Warren, B., Ogonowski, M., & Ballenger, C. (2005). The generative potential of students' everyday knowledge in learning science. In T. Carpenter & T. Romberg (Eds.), *Understanding matters: Improving student learning in mathematics and science* (pp. 55–80). Mahwah, NJ: Erlbaum.

Rosen, L. (2000). *Calculating concerns: The politics or representation in California's "Math Wars."* Unpublished doctoral dissertation. University of California, San Diego.

Schoenfeld, A. H. (2004). The math wars. *Educational Policy, 18*(1), 253–286. Schoenfeld, A. H. (2008a). Mathematics for understanding. In L. Darling-Hammond, B. Barron, P. D. Pearson, A. H. Schoenfeld, T. Zimmerman, G. Cervetti, & J. Tilson. *Powerful learning* (pp. 113–150). San Francisco: Jossey-Bass.

Schoenfeld, A. H. (2008b). Problem Solving in The United States, 1970–2008: Research and Theory, Practice and Politics. In G. Tomer, A. H. Schoenfeld, & K. Reiss (Eds.). *Problem solving around the world— Summing up the state of the art.* Special issue of the Zentralblatt fiir Didaktik der Mathematik: Issue I, 2008.

Schoenfeld, A. H. (2009). Working with schools: The story of a mathematics education collaboration. *American Mathematical Monthly, 116*(3), 197–217.

Schoenfeld, A. H. (2010). *How we think: A theory of goal-oriented decision making and its educational applications.* New York: Routledge.

Senk, S. L., & Thompson, D. R. (Eds.) (2003). *Standards-based school mathematics curricula: What are they? What do students learn?* Mahwah, NJ: Erlbaum.

Stolberg, S. G. (2011, February 17). Shy U.S. intellectual created playbook used in a revolution. *New York Times,* p 1. Downloaded, February 17, 2011, from <http://www.nytimes.com/2011102117/world/middleeast/17sharp.html?_r=1 &sq=sheryl%20g ay%20stolberg&st=cse&adxnnl=J &scp=2&adxnnlx= J297969311- Y!NtLp/sDXbQKctRVetbfw>

Stylianides, A. (2005). *Proof in school mathematics classrooms: Developing a conceptualization of its meaning and investigating what is entailed in its cultivation.* Unpublished dissertation, University of Michigan.

Tomer, G., Schoenfeld, A. H., & Reiss, K. (Eds.). (2008) *Problem solving around the world—Summing up the state of the art.* Special issue of the Zentralblatt für Didaktik der Mathematik, 39(5–6). Issue 1, 2008.

Warren, B., & Rosebery, A. (1995). Equity in the future tense: Redefining relationships among teachers, students, and science in linguistic minority classrooms. In W. Secada, E. Fennema, & L. Adajian (Eds.), *New directions for equity in mathematics education* (pp. 298–328). NY: Cambridge University Press.

CHAPTER 10

EDUCATING
THE WHOLE CHILD

Intellect, Emotion, and Spirit, With Wisdom and Passion

Barbara Day
University of North Carolina

Elizabeth De Gaynor
Duke Divinity School

If the sacred and the secular cannot be disentangled, and if (much) secular thought is in fact hostile to religion (rather than neutral), and if religion can be rational, or if secular thought is a matter of ideological commitments or faith, then the conventional wisdom of modern American education is profoundly mistaken.

—Nord, 1995, p. 7

A basic premise of holistic education is the belief that our lives have a meaning and purpose greater than the mechanistic laws described by science, and greater than the 'consensus consciousness' of any one creature. This transcendent purpose is a creative, self-guiding energy which we ought not attempt to suppress. No ideology, no social order devised by wealth or power-seeking factions should be allowed to corrupt the delicate, miraculous unfolding of this

Schooling for Tomorrow's America, pages 129–147
Copyright © 2014 by Information Age Publishing
All rights of reproduction in any form reserved.

creative energy. Ultimately, a spiritual worldview is a reverence for life, an attitude of wonder and awe in the face of the transcendent source of our being.

—(Miller, 1990, p. 154)

We begin with a number of presuppositions about the role spirituality should have in educating the whole child.[1] We believe that human beings have mental, emotional, physical, and spiritual facets; they are not simply brains attached to skeletal sticks. Educating the "whole" person requires addressing all of those components. We believe spirituality has a place in the public school classroom (legally and ethically) because it matters to most Americans. Determining the dimensions of that place requires knowing the Constitutional boundaries and understanding specific educational communities. America has always been a place in which religion and spirituality interact with educational and civic goals. Throughout our history, we have (re) negotiated the terms of the relationship between them. The twenty-first century is ripe to reconsider the relationship yet again. Our goal is to allow human beings to be individually re-integrated (mind/body/spirit) and socially re-constituted into spiritually aware and spiritually open educational communities.

In this chapter, we will identify issues related to spirituality and education, including:

1. When spirituality is sidelined in the classroom, students and communities suffer because they are denied an area of the self that matters deeply to them.
2. We can use lessons from history to shape the place of spirituality in education.
3. The *telos* of education matters greatly because it shapes the kind of students who are formed by the system. Rather than aiming for students with high tests scores, we hope for well-rounded citizens.
4. Spirituality should be part of holistic education, but its implementation will look different at various educational levels. We offer suggestions for elementary through high school.

WHY DO WE NEED TO GIVE SPIRITUALITY A PLACE IN THE CLASSROOM?

An extensive survey by the Pew Forum on Religion & Public Life details statistics on religion in America and explores the shifts taking place in the U.S. religious landscape. Based on interviews with more than 35,000 Americans age 18 and older, this 2007 survey found that, although religious affiliation in the United States is both very diverse and extremely fluid, 71% of

Americans believe in God and 56% of Americans say that religion is "very important" in their lives. As such, we cannot pretend that spiritual and religious beliefs do not matter. Smith and Dean's *Soul Searching* (2005) details data gleaned from random phone surveys and interviews of teenagers in the United States (*National Study of Youth and Religion, 2001–2005* at the University of North Carolina). The authors argue that to comprehend adequately the lives of American young people is "to understand their religious and spiritual beliefs, commitments, practices, experiences, and desires" (Smith & Dean, 2005, p. 4). They note that

> About half of U.S. teenagers report in their survey answers strong subjective importance and experiences of religious faith in their own lives, measured as importance of faith, closeness to God, commitment of life to God, experience of powerful worship, answer to prayer, lack of religious doubts, and receiving guidance from God. (p. 68)

There is a positive association between religious involvement and positive outcomes in life, seen in multiple areas: "risk behaviors, quality of family and adult relationships, moral reasoning and behavior, community participation, media consumption, sexual activity, and emotional well-being" (Smith & Dean, 2005, p. 218). Young people who are serious about religious faith and practice are better off across the board and "the greater the supply of religiously grounded relationships, activities, programs, opportunities, and challenges available to teenagers, other things being equal, the more likely teenagers will be religiously engaged and invested" (Smith & Dean, 2005, p. 261).

Although teens' religious and spiritual lives are significant to them, this aspect often goes unexplored and undiscussed, especially at school. One result is that teens' ability to articulate their beliefs varies widely and most are nearly inarticulate on the topic. Even if schools are not perceived to be hostile to religion, students keep expressions of religious faith to a minimum while at school. It is possible, however, for public schools to help students address spiritual matters in ways that are civil and inclusive.

WHAT CAN WE LEARN FROM YESTERDAY'S AMERICA?

As Secretary of the Massachusetts Board of Education (1837–1848), Horace Mann clearly recognized the importance of education and its role in communities, particularly in a nation that was striving to define and unify itself. He believed well-educated children would be good citizens. He understood

> That in a nation without a single established church, some new institution needed to step in to fill the void. Some force had to continue the process of

shaping and carrying the common culture and morality if there was to be a unified people. (Fraser, 1999, p. 31)[2]

In America, that unifying institution could be public education. Mann believed common schools should provide religious education in a general and tolerant way, allowing each child to make an informed, free choice about which form of religion to adopt. Religious education would help individuals overcome "moral oscillation" and would connect people through shared experience. According to Mann, moral education is at the center of smooth, civil existence. "Education, then, beyond all other devices of human origin, is the great equalizer of the conditions of men [sic]—the balance wheel of the social machinery" (Mann, 1872, p. 707).

He warned that "the unrestrained passions of men are not only homicidal, but suicidal; and community without a conscience would soon extinguish itself" (Mann, 1872, p .701). Morality, he believed, is best found in religion, and human beings are meant to be religious:

> *Devoid* of religious principles and religious affections, the race can never fall so low but that it may sink still lower; animated and sanctified by them, it can never rise so high but that it may ascend still higher...Indeed, the whole frame and constitution of the human soul, show, that if man [sic] be not a religious being, he is among the most deformed and *monstrous* of all possible existences. His propensities and passions need the fear of God, as a restraint from evil; and his sentiments and affections need the love of God as a condition and preliminary to ever thing worthy of the name of happiness. (Mann, 1872, p. 710)

Notice how his description of "religious being" is similar to current definitions of "spirituality." According to this position, people who believe that the human race can attain happiness or avoid misery without religion are ignorant about human nature.

Mann gives the reader a brief history lesson about how governments have attempted "to secure the prevalence and permanence of religion among the people," (Mann, 1872, p. 723) explaining that there are basically two systems of such activities. The first, which has prevailed for 1500 years, "holds the regulation and control of the religious belief of the people to be one of the functions of government, like the command of the army or navy, or the establishment of courts, or the collections of revenues" (Mann, 1872, p. 723). The second holds that "belief is a matter of individual and parental concern; and while the government furnishes all practicable facilities for the independent formation of that belief, it exercises no authority to prescribe or coercion to enforce it" (Mann, 1872, p. 723). Government in the latter system facilitates the acquisition of religious truth, but does not arbitrate what religious truth actually is. Mann cites the Constitution of

Massachusetts as an expression of this precept: "All religious sects and denominations, demeaning themselves peaceably and as good citizens, shall be equally under the protection of law; and no subordination of one sect or denomination to another shall ever be established by law" (Mann, 1872, p. 723). He also commends the United States as "a solitary example among the nations of the earth, where freedom of opinions and the inviolability of conscience have been even theoretically recognized by the law" (Mann, 1872, p. 717, 723). In laying out his description of the resultant religious education, he explains that it should proceed in broad and general ways, "leaving it to every individual to add, for himself, those auxiliary arguments which may result from his own peculiar views of religious truth" (Mann, 1972, p. 714–715).

Mann agrees that public schools are not seminaries and should be restricted from teaching "the peculiar and distinctive doctrines of any religious denomination" (Mann, 1872, p. 729). They should "acknowledge their limitations and inculcate 'Christian Morals' founded in the Bible. But in using the Bible, it must "speak for itself" without the use of sectarian glasses/interpretations" (Mann, 1872, p. 729). There should be no protest to its use in this way, Mann avers that

> . . . in all my intercourse for twelve years, whether personal or by letter, with all the school officers in the State, and with tens of thousands of individuals in it, I have never heard an objection made to use of the Bible in school except in one or two instances, and, in those cases, the objection was put upon the ground, that daily familiarity with the book, in school, would tend to impair a reverence for it. (Mann, 1872, p. 735)

As we can see in Catholic opposition to common schools, Mann's assertion of *sola scriptura* is a distinctively Protestant approach.[3] Mann goes on to assert that a system "whose first and cardinal principle it is to recognize and protect the highest and dearest of all human interests, and of all human rights" cannot be "an irreligious, and anti-Christian, or an un-Christian one (Mann, 1872, p. 731). Although Mann was correct that people care about the intersection of religion and education, he was oblivious regarding possible objections, both from non-Unitarian denominations and from those of other religious groups. We believe it is possible to allow diverse religious views to be presented in school without any of them being given primacy.

WHAT CAN WE SUGGEST FOR TODAY'S AMERICA?

Warren Nord notes that religion has been and continues to be central to American culture and, therefore, must have a place in education. Nord argues that neither restoration of unilateral "religious purposes, practices and teaching to public education" nor their removal into the private realm is an appropriate response (Nord, 1995, p. xiii). He argues that educators must take religion seriously (a position supported by the First Amendment), but this can be done without endorsement of or indoctrination into any one particular religion. Charles Hanes and Oliver Thomas wrote *Finding Common Ground: A Guide to Religious Liberty in Public Schools* as a manual for teachers, administrators, and parents. They indicate that religion has played a significant historical and social role and is essential to understanding the nation and the world. Omission of facts about religion can encourage students to develop the false impression that the religious life of humankind is insignificant or unimportant. "Failure to understand even the basic symbols, practices, and concepts of the various religions makes much of history, literature, art, and contemporary life unintelligible. Moreover, knowledge of the roles of religion in the past and present promotes cross cultural understanding essential to democracy and world peace" (Hanes & Thomas, 2001, p. 43).[4] They suggest that religion should be studied where it "naturally arises" and differentiate what can be taught in elementary grades (e.g., learning about family, community, culture, etc.), and in secondary grades, addressed through literature, social studies, art, and other electives, using primary sources.[5]

WHAT KIND OF PEOPLE DO WE WANT OUR EDUCATIONAL SYSTEM TO FORM? SHIFTING OUR FOCUS

By the latter part of the nineteenth century, the values that America praised were industry and frugality, and as the ideology of the Enlightenment reached their shores, theology and moral philosophy were replaced by the overriding values of individualism, pragmatism, and empiricism. The sacred was separated from the secular and education became more utilitarian. Some argue that these developments have led to mechanized and economic models of education. In March 2009, as part of his first 100 days in office, President Obama spoke about the state of education and his vision for its improvement:

> The source of America's prosperity has never been merely how ably we accumulate wealth, but how well we educate our people … The future belongs to the nation that best educates its citizens … And yet, despite resources that are unmatched anywhere in the world, we've let our grades slip, our schools crumble, our teacher quality fall short, and other nations outpace us … It's not that their kids are any smarter than ours—it's that they are being smarter about how to educate their children. They're spending less time teaching things that don't matter, and more time teaching things that

do. They're preparing their students not only for high school or college, but for a career. (Remarks to Hispanic Chamber of Commerce, March 10. 2009 available at http://www.nytimes.com/2009/03/10/us/politics/10test-obama.html)

Notice how his words are couched in terms of competition (us vs. them) and notice the connection he draws between subjects learned and success achieved. The goal is the production of citizens who will be prepared to prosper as workers in the global economy.[6] In the search for results, President Obama said he was

> . . . calling on our nation's governors and state education chiefs to develop standards and assessments that don't simply measure whether students can fill in a bubble on a test, but whether they possess twenty-first century skills like problem-solving, and critical thinking, and entrepreneurship, and creativity. (Remarks to Hispanic Chamber of Commerce, March 10, 2009 available at http://www.nytimes.com/2009/03/10/us/politics/10test-obama.html)

He is right to move beyond standardized tests into the realms of critical thinking and creativity, but nowhere in the speech is transformation of entire persons (mind/body/soul) mentioned as a goal, nor is spirituality suggested as a foundation or a driving force in their education. Although he is correct about the centrality of education in the formation of people, some would disagree with him about which things "matter" and with his proposed *telos*.

LOOKING AT EDUCATION THROUGH A DIFFERENT LENS

James Smith (2009) asks many questions about the purpose of education.

> What if education . . . is not primarily about absorption of ideas and information, but about the formation of hearts and desires? . . . What if the primary work of education was the transforming of our imagination rather than the saturation of our intellect? What if education wasn't first and foremost about what we know, but about what we love? (p. 18)

He defines education as "a holistic endeavor that involves the whole person, including our bodies, in a process of formation that aims our desires, primes our imagination, and orients us to the world—all before we start *thinking* about it" (2009, p. 39). He asserts that there is no neutral, non-formative education. Behind every curriculum, behind every set of educational practices, and behind every teacher's pedagogy is a philosophical/theological anthropology, a set of assumptions about the nature of being human and a particular vision of the good life. Unfortunately, too many educators have accepted that human beings are primarily thinking entities, which is closely related to Enlightenment and Modern constructions. The goal of education should not be merely to have a wealth of knowledge, but also to develop an intuitive understanding of the world.

Nicholas Wolterstorff asserts that school curriculum

> ...must be set by reference to what one is aiming at with respect to the students... [it] must be of worth and significance to students in their lives outside the school as well as inside... it must be undertaken for the sake of life as a whole. (2002, p. 20)

If he is correct, then we must attend to students as holistic beings in a given context. Elliot Eisner agrees: "There can be no adequate conception of appropriate curriculum content without consideration of the context in which it is to be provided and students for whom it is intended" (1994, p. 106).[7] In his book, *Educational Imagination*, Eisner describes the explicit curriculum (goals which are publicly stated), the implicit curriculum (goals which are valued, but not explicitly stated) and the null curriculum (things schools do not teach).[8] It is the null set that interests us here, because spirituality/religion/faith has been an area of inquiry which has been avoided in public schools. Eisner is right that this omission has consequences:

> Ignorance is not simply a neutral void: it has important effects on the kinds of options one is available to consider, the alternatives one can examine, and the perspectives from which one can view a situation or problems. (Eisner, 1994, p. 97)

Eisner supports reform in education to focus on holistic teaching and learning. Caring for the whole child means recognizing students' individual talents, addressing more than just the cognitive, finding more holistic and meaningful forms of assessment, and valuing the social and emotional life of the child. Eisner suggests that progressive educators gave us a holistic education vision, but he contends that the emphasis on boosting test scores and standardizing outcomes has narrowed the curriculum and dimmed our vision of what educators, influenced by John Dewey's philosophy of education, used to call the "whole child." If we focus all of our attention on measuring academic performance, we neglect the social and emotional development of our students which are so important in living satisfying lives.

How did we get to such a narrow view of our educational system? Eisner thinks it has to do with an historical perspective with the Industrial Revolution leading the way—a way of thinking about productivity that uses systematic control to achieve high levels of predictability. A second reason, he says, is the desire to make comparative analysis possible in our approaches to school reform. If a district uses the same curriculum, with the same standards, the same evaluation practices and testing programs, then we may have comparative data about student performance in each of our school systems or districts. We live in a competitive culture; schools often focus on what will boost test scores, not necessarily what is best for students. The results, according to Eisner, are myriad: "Cheating increases, the curriculum narrows, and the reward system undermines any intrinsic satisfaction that students might secure from their work in school" (Eisner, 2005, p. 14–18). High stakes testing is one example of this competitive rationality; however, it is the general ethos created by a technical orientation that values effectiveness and efficiency and downplays spiritual imagination or social awareness.

Nel Noddings points out that

> ...a democratic society demands much more of its schools than producing graduates who are proficient in reading and mathematics. It demands graduates who exhibit sound character, the ability to think critically, a social conscience, willingness to make commitments, awareness of global problems, and ability to make wise civic choices. Education policy must address these aims to meet the needs of both individuals and society. (Noddings, 2005, p. 8–13)

She asserts that teachers must introduce students to the world and help them to live competently and morally in that world. This goal requires presence and relationships and acknowledgement of the moral overtones in teaching. In the area of religion, students should be exposed to information and its affective accompaniments:

> They should have opportunities to feel what the other is feeling as a result of deeply held belief. They should be touched by beauty, faith, and devotion manifested in the religious practices of others. Through such experiences—feeling with the other in spiritual responsiveness—they may be reconnected to each other in caring. (Noddings, 1984, p. 185)

Noddings defines moral education as the approach of the educator to content that "enhances the ethical ideal of those being educated so that they will continue to meet others morally" (1984, p. 171). We must examine our lives carefully, including reflection on our relationship to culture and community, and this may lead to controversy. Without this kind of tension, however, our thinking is weakened. Dialogue is crucial and all topics of intellectual inquiry must be fair game.[9] Schools should be places where beliefs can be examined with charity and critique. There are questions that every thoughtful human being asks, and to avoid them is "educational malpractice," because "a longing for the sacred persists and there is widespread ignorance on religious matters" (Noddings, 2006, p. 278). Noddings uses findings from *Soul Searching* to note that students are interested and invested in spirituality, but unfortunately are inarticulate about their faith, in part because so few adults have engaged in conversation with them about these issues. Students should have a basic vocabulary about religion/faith/God. Introducing students to a wide range of views offers opportunities for reflection and conversation.

Parker Palmer suggests that "when we bring forth the spirituality of teaching and learning, we help students honor life's most meaningful questions." He makes it clear that as he explores ways to "evoke the spirit in education, "he wants "neither to violate the separation of church and state nor to encourage people who would impose their religious beliefs on others" (Palmer, 1998, p. 4).

And yet, he is also passionate about caring for the deepest needs of the soul, which education often neglects. For example, when teachers dispense facts at the expense of meaning and information at the expense of wisdom, they create a system that alienates us. Our real questions, Palmer argues, are often largely in our hearts. We fear asking them in front of others. Students want to connect with questions about life: "Does my life have meaning and purpose?" "Do I have gifts that the world needs and wants?" "What and who can I trust?" "How do I deal with suffering—my own and that of my family and friends?" Instead, we ask questions like, "What's on the test tomorrow?" "How do I go about getting a raise?" Students need and want facts and formulas; they also need compassion and companionship.

Palmer asserts that North American institutions of learning are (de) formed by individualism, empiricism, and competition; we are left with a "cosmology of fragmentation" (1983, p. xiv). We can trace the roots of disintegration to the Enlightenment, which separated the unity of knowing and being and reduced the human desire for truth and wisdom to a quest for rational certainty. Palmer describes one resulting approach to learning as *objectivism*. It pushes us to distance ourselves from the things we want to know because we believe they must be known from afar. Power rests with those at the top who have the most objectively detached understanding, and education is a system of delivering observations as facts to be passively accepted and repeated by students. Palmer explains that this approach turns the focus outward, neglecting the inner reality of the learner, when knowledge should be an interaction of fact and passions. The other side of the objectivist coin is *subjectivism*, a form of pluralism in which each person's perceptions of truth cannot be challenged by another's insomuch as all perceptions are held to be equally valid. This approach "isolates the self, creates as many worlds as there are knowers, destroys the possibility of community, and finally makes the other an object of real account" (Palmer, 1983, p. 55).

What we need, according to Palmer, is *wholesight*, where mind and heart are united and we accept that knowing requires connection with the subject and is acquired in community.[10] This claim is not simply for a therapeutic community with intimacy as its aim, or a civic community with mere tolerance/civility as its aim. Instead, engagement must be intellectually rigorous, and this position "requires an ethos of trust and acceptance … [and] depends on things like honest dissent and the willingness to change our minds"(Palmer, 1983, p. xvii). Palmer suggests that education should offer truth, not merely facts, theories, or objectives as a way to counteract the will to power. "In truthful knowing we neither infuse the world with our subjectivity (as pre-modern knowing did) nor hold it at arm's length, manipulating it to suit our needs (as is the modern style)" (Palmer 1983, p. 32). Our knowledge should spring from compassion/love, as opposed to a desire to control. Palmer reminds us that neither teaching nor learning can be done by "disembodied intellects but by whole persons whose minds cannot be disconnected from feeling and spirit, from heart and soul" (Palmer, 1998–1999, p. 10).

As we consider various ways of knowing, Palmer reminds us that "knowledge contains it own morality, it begins not in a neutrality but in a place of passion within the human soul. Depending on the nature of that passion, our knowledge will follow certain courses and head toward certain ends" (Palmer, 1983, p. 7). Palmer shatters the illusion teachers have of objectivity or detachment, because "as I teach, I project the condition of my soul onto my students, my subject, and our way of being together … teaching holds a mirror to the soul" (Palmer, 1998, p. 2). Educational reform begins with teachers and their self-awareness of the forces that drive their knowing, as these are the same forces that will drive their teaching.

> Reduce teaching to intellect, and it becomes a cold abstraction; reduce it to emotions, and it becomes narcissistic; reduce it to the spiritual, and it loses its anchor to the world. Intellect, emotion, and spirit depend on one another for wholeness. (Palmer, 1983, p. 4)

In *To Know as We are Known* and *The Courage to Teach*, Palmer develops paradoxical principles of pedagogy, asserting that the education space should be: bounded and open; charged and hospitable; inviting to the voice of the individual and the voice of the group; honoring to the little stories of students and the big stories of disciplines and traditions; supporting of solitude and surrounded by community; and welcoming to both speech and silence.

HOW DOES SPIRITUALITY FIT WITH INITIATIVES CONCERNED WITH THE HOLISTIC EDUCATION?

Holistic education is about educating the whole child, mentally, emotionally, morally, physically, psychologically, spiritually, and artistically. Educating the whole child is based on an understanding that each one of us finds meaning and purpose (and our own identity) in life as we become connected to each other, our community, our natural world, and to spiritual values such as peace and compassion. The goal in the education of the whole child is for our students to have an intrinsic reverence for life and a love of learning that is passionate.

Today, an urgent need exists for positive social change that creates a better world through cooperation and collaboration rather than competition and conflict. We must provide the type of education which calls forth a development of each person as a whole. Our students are spiritual beings capable of becoming intelligent, ethical, and responsible, able to cooperate effectively and peaceful in solving problems (Hubbard, 2011, np). Kathleen Kesson laments that "for too long the inner world of children has been suppressed or denied, and this is a serious flaw in our educational thinking" (Kesson, 1993, p. 3). Educating the whole child is a natural remedy.

The whole child paradigm places the role of the teacher as a "facilitator of learning" who understands the psychological value of creativity and the productivity of work. "The cultivation of creative intelligence depends on the freedom to engage in active experiential learning motivated by natural curiosity of inquiry" (Kesson, 1993, p. 4). The facilitating teacher prepares a learning environment which respects the wide range of diverse needs, including basic psychological needs, the need for security and self-esteem, as well as higher psychological needs, such as the need for spiritual growth. The complex aspects of the total human personality must be developed—physical, emotional, intellectual, psychological, social, political, creative, artistic, philosophical, and spiritual.

The Association for Supervision and Curriculum Development (ASCD) recognizes that today's educational practices and policies have focused too much on academic achievement. They want that to change with recognition that students must not only be knowledgeable when they graduate, but they must also be emotionally, physically, healthy, civically engaged, responsible and caring human beings. ASCD has launched a new initiative called, "The Whole Child Action Agenda." The initiative advocates a comprehensive approach to teaching and learning. The position statement promotes the belief that every child deserves a twenty-first century education that supports the development of a person who is "healthy, safe, engaged, supported, and challenged" (http//www.wholechildeducation.org, 10/27/11) Let us hope (and believe) that ASCD's Whole Child Initiative will be a guiding force in leading us into the best that we can become for twenty-first century schooling.

WHAT CAN WE LEARN
FROM EARLY CHILDHOOD EDUCATORS?

Many teachers, especially early childhood educators, have embraced the "whole child" way of teaching and learning for many years. They have explored development/experiential methods as the natural way that young children learn. Their classrooms offer inviting, encouraging, active exploration and "hands on" learning. They believe in sound child development principles that meet the needs of the whole child:

1. Children grow and develop at unique, individual rates that are often unrelated to chronological age. (Many learning activities at a variety of challenge levels should be provided in an effort to meet the needs of all children. Even within the range of preoperational learning there are many levels.)
2. Children are free to follow many of their natural interests.
3. Learning is what children do; it is not something that is done to them. (The child must be directly involved in doing the learning. Telling the child may result in empty verbalizations.)
4. Play is the child's way of working and learning. (Children acquire many skills through play. They try new roles, solve problems, learn how to make sense of the environment, and practice social skills.)
5. Children learn many things from each other, including respect for themselves and others ways of learning how to learn, and a sense of responsibility and achievement (Bloom, 1981).
6. A specially constructed, rich learning environment, filled with concrete and sensory learning materials, is essential in helping children to learn. (The environment is the vehicle for learning, and it must provide the materials the child needs for exploration and learning.)
7. The integrated day, involving centers-oriented, simultaneously occurring activities within the learning environment, is one of the creative approaches to the development of basic skills. (Life is a spectrum of all types of overlapping skills, and activities. An integrated approach helps the child to see how the newly acquired skills fit into a broader realm of experiences, thus providing a reason for learning. Children can see how learning "school skills" will help them in everyday life.)
8. In a learning atmosphere based on trust and structure freedom, children are encouraged to use their own initiative and to be self-reliant.

(Children need reassurance and security but they also need intriguing challenge. They need and respond to praise for a job well done.)

9. The uniqueness of the child, as reflected in his or her individuality and learning style, should be appreciated and valued.

10. Young children are experiencing rapid and important development in many areas; cognitive-intellectual, psychosocial, and physical-motor. An appropriate program supports development in all areas, rather than focusing solely on cognitive development (Day, 1988, pp. 16–17).

WHAT CAN WE LEARN FROM EDUCATORS IN SECONDARY SCHOOLS?

High school professionals have also worked for many years to move toward a more holistic model. Educating the whole child requires differentiation for a variety of student learning preferences. If we believe that students have different learning styles and learn in a variety of ways, then teachers obviously must embrace methods of education that respond to these various styles of learning. And, if we add the component of spirituality into the mix of mentally, socially, morally, physically, and so forth, we have the richest teaching and learning imaginable. Let us imagine it through the lens of a teacher who sees her essential understanding of spiritually being articulated into classroom priorities (S. Stack, *Bringing Spirituality into our Schools*, Unpublished essay):

1. Sense of Journey—most students can explore subject content as a journey. Students can reflect of the nature of journeys [the key elements or unifying principles (quest, goals, companions/allies, trails, enigmas, obstacles overcome, discipline, mastery, peaks achieved, celebration sharing, renewal) and the sense of purpose, adventure, disaster, survival, resilience, going deep within self] and compare these to the journeys in their lives.

2. Inner Practices—students can be given the opportunity to experience different types of inner practices (mindfulness, love, contemplation, connection, reflection) to get a sense of what they do for them, and to have choices in their practice. Examples could include
   - practices of stillness and contemplation;
   - guided visualizations in creative writings to spur imagination and to generate questions;
   - using stories that engage the emotions to help students connect fully to the topic (Role plays/drama/hypothetical which connect

students to phenomena or different perspective—using hear, mind, body and soul); and
- collaborative activities which enable deep relationship connections.
3. Service, Ethical Practice, and Vocation—exploring what it means to develop generosity, justice, democracy, pluralism, ethical freedom, and wisdom—finding stories with the topic that exemplify the process and the issues, using role plays, journaling dialogue.
4. Inspiring students to all that is best in humanity, encouraging idealism. Providing opportunities for students to do things for others, whether inside a group or for other communities, enabling them to learn fully from such experiences, reflecting on the nature of relationships, how outcomes related to purposes. Encouraging and helping them to develop their own code of ethics which they apply to their own practice. Helping them discover the reflexivity between inner and outer purposes, helping them to discover within themselves a sense of vocation and purpose.
5. Self-Expression—encouraging students to draw deeply from themselves and invest in what they do; valuing uniqueness and heartfeltness; balancing this with the need for technical advancement.
6. Conflict, Inner Crisis, and Transformation—finding in the subject content stories which illustrate the nature of conflict, crisis, and transformation and relating these back to students' own conflict situations in their lives. Using conflict situations that arise naturally as opportunities to explore different approaches and reflect on outcomes. For example, much advancement in science occurs as a result of an anomaly—a phenomenon in direct conflict to the current ways of thinking. By exploring this process and relating it to how our own ways of thinking and knowing are perturbed, students gain awareness at a metacognitive level that can help them better understand and deal with what they are going through.
7. Inquiry Process—the inquiry process involves deep questions, little questions, searching for answers, exploring finding out, test, experiencing, gaining evidence or feedback, reflecting, seeking patterns and meaning, evaluating, hypothesizing, imagining, using intuition, feelings, logic, seeking plausibility at many levels, theorizing, connecting with and to others, comparing, discussing, looking for the big picture, looking for emergent understanding, looking at the little picture, applying, determining usefulness and appropriateness, understanding the paradigm you are in and the limitations of it. This inquiry is motivated by a thirst for understanding, a sense of wonder.

Trilling reminds us that questions have long been the method for discovering new knowledge, and problems have been the inspiration for investing new ways to live and work—methods long used (but not often enough), yet proven to work are inquiry (question-based) and design (problem-based) approaches. These methods offer students time to analyze their thought processes and increase their motivation and engagement, that which Parker Palmer earlier called soulful or spiritual learning (Trilling, 2010, pp. 8–11).

From historical, legal, and ethical perspectives, religion has a place in schools, and creating a space for the spiritual elements of learning is appropriate and necessary. We remain hopeful that educators and supporting stakeholders will strive to find ways to address all of the learning needs of their students in order to educate the whole child.

NOTES

1. There is wide variety in defining spirituality and religion. Parker Palmer depicts spirituality as "the ancient and abiding human quest for connectedness with something larger and more trustworthy than our egos with our own souls, with one another, with the worlds of history and nature, with the invisible winds of the spirit, with the mystery of being alive" (Palmer, 1998, p. 6). Warren Nord notes that religion is a modern term because it "names one aspect of life among many. We take religions to be discrete institutions and systems of belief which stand alongside scientific and political and economic institutions and ideas." This is in contrast to pre-modern visions of the world in which all was connected (Nord, 1995, p. 16). We do not share this sense of distinction, nor are we afraid of students and teachers acknowledging their religious subject position in conversations. It is our contention that spirituality and religion are not easily separable and that in most cases, the former is enacted by practicing/embodying the latter. For this chapter, we will use spirituality to denote one component of human being, and we will use religion to denote one place where that component is fostered.

2. Fraser goes on to suggest that Mann was like other educational reformers (Samuel Lewis and Calvin Stowe in Ohio, John Pierce in Michigan, Caleb Mills in Indiana, and Henry Barnard in Connecticut) who proposed a non-sectarian (Protestant) Christian educational system that would be "so effective in building and transmitting a common culture that only the minor details had to be left to the different denominational educational efforts" (Fraser, 1999, p. 39).

3. One noteworthy example of Protestantism was the 1869 resolution by the National Teachers Association to read the Bible devotionally, but without comment by the teachers. Nord wisely notes that both the Bible and the reading methodology (without commentary of traditional church teaching) used was Protestant (*Religion and American Education*, 73). Amy Simpson and others have noted the ways that Christian privilege remains implicitly pervasive in American public schools.

4. They summarize the ways religion should be taught: The school's approach to religion is *academic*, not *devotional*; The school strives for student *awareness* of

religions, but does not press for student *acceptance* of any religion; The school sponsors study *about* religion, not the *practice* of religion; The school may *expose* students to a diversity of religious views, but may not *impose* any particular view; The school *educates* about all religions; it does not *promote* or *denigrate* religion; The school *informs* students about various beliefs; it does not seek to *conform* students to any particular belief.

5. Elementary and Secondary education are not the same thing, and their unique realities require a different approach to integrating spirituality in the classroom. For example, the power differential between elementary students and their teachers is often greater than that found between secondary students and their teachers. As such, the latter are less likely to be proselytized simply by knowing the spiritual/religious beliefs of those who educate them or those with whom they learn.

6. bell hooks asserts that the classroom is not an assembly line (hooks, 1994; *Teaching to Transgress*, 13), and Paulo Freire denounces the dominant banking model of education as "either misguided or mistrusting of people" (Freire, 2009; *Pedagogy of the Oppressed*, 79). He counters it with "democratic proposals of problem-posing education" (12, 72–74).

7. According to Paolo Freire, human beings are not "abstract, isolated, independent, and unattached to the world." (*Pedagogy of the Oppressed*, 81). We are defined and shaped by our contexts, although these structural forces are often invisible. It is the task of education to uncover our perceptual blind spots.

8. The *implicit* curriculum can be seen in school architecture and the design of furniture. Eisner explains that buildings "express the values we cherish, and, once built, they reinforce those values. Schools are educational churches, and our gods, judging from the altars we build, are economy and efficiency" (97).

9. Paolo Freire would agree about the power of dialogue, which he defined as an encounter between people, mediated by the world in order to name the world, that leads to liberatory praxis ["the action and reflection upon the world in order to transform it"] (*Pedagogy of the Oppressed*, 79). In Panama City, Florida, Rutherford High School has a number of clubs, including a new one for atheists. Students (atheists, agnostics, and Christians) at the school are engaged in conversations and activities about religious faith (and the lack thereof), and they are managing to do so without seeking conversion, controversy, or undue contention. They have created safe spaces for conversation about faith commitments and are offering opportunities to know one another. (Michael Wincrip (April 3, 2011). "Teenagers Speak Up for Lack of Faith." *New York Times*).

10. bell hooks would agree that the classroom should be a community where everyone's presence is acknowledged and all participants are empowered to speak and to listen, but the community must acknowledge difference and the ways knowing is "forged in history and relations of power." It's not about denying the presence of power dynamics in the classroom, but about deciding how power is disseminated within the classroom (*Teaching to Transgress*, 8 and 30).

REFERENCES

ASCD, 2011. http://www.wholechildeducation.org

Bloom, B. S. (1981). *All our children learning: A primer for parents, teachers, and other educators.* NY: McGraw-Hill.

Day, B. (1988). *Early childhood education: Creative learning activities.* (3rd ed.) NY: Macmillan.

Day, B. (1999). *Teaching and learning in the new millennium.* Indianapolis, IN: Kappa Delta Pi International Honor Society.

Eisner, E. (2005). Back to whole. *Educational Leadership, 63*(1), 14–18.

Eisner, E. (1994). The three curricula that all schools teach. *The educational imagination: On the design and evaluation of school programs* (3rd ed.) NY: Macmillan.

Fraser, J. W. (1999). *Between church and state: Religion and public education in a multicultural America.* NY: St. Martin's Press.

Freire, P. (2009). *Pedagogy of the oppressed* (30th Anniversary Edition). New York: Continuum.

Haynes, C., & Thomas, O. (2001). *Finding common ground: A guide to religious liberty in public schools.* First Amendment Center.

hooks, b. (1994). *Teaching to transgress: Education as the practice of freedom.* New York: Routledge.

Hubbard, M. (2011). *Future schools and education as the practice of freedom for growth through learning: 'Holistic Education.'* http://www.holistic.educator.com

Kesson, K. (1993). Critical theory and holistic education: Carrying on the conversation, the renewal of meaning in education. In R. Miller (Ed.), *Responses to the cultural and ecological crisis of our times.* Brandon, VT: Holistic Education Press.

Mann, H. (1872). *Annual reports on education.* M.T. Mann (Ed), Boston: Lee and Shepard. Accessed via Google Books: http://books.google.com/books?id=1 Dk4AAAAYAAJ&source=gbs_navlinks_s

Miller, R. (1990). *What are schools for? Holistic education in American culture.* Brandon, VT: Holistic Education Press.

Noddings, N. (1984). *Caring: A feminine approach to ethics and moral education.* Berkeley: University of California Press.

Noddings, N. (2005, September). What does it mean to educate the whole child? *Educational Leadership, 63*(1):8–13.

Noddings, N. (2006). *Critical lessons: What our schools should teach.* New York, NY: Cambridge.

Nord, W. A. (1995). *Religion and American education: Rethinking a national dilemma.* Chapel Hill, NC: University of North Carolina Press.

Obama, B. President Obama's Remarks to the Hispanic Chamber of Commerce. Washington, DC, 10 March 2009. http://www.nytimes.com/2009/03/10/us/politics/10text-obama.html

Palmer, P. (1998, December–1999, January). Evoking the spirit in public education. *Educational Leadership. 56*(4).

Palmer, P (1998). *The courage to teach: Exploring the inner landscape of a teacher's life.* San Francisco: Jossey-Bass.

Palmer, P. (1983). *To know as we are known: Education as a spiritual journey.* New York, NY: Harper.

Pew Forum on Religion and Public Life: US Religious Landscape Survey (2007). http://religions.pewforum.org

Smith, C., & Dean, M. L. (2005). *Soul searching: The religious and spiritual lives of American teenagers.* New York, NY: Oxford University Press.

Smith, J. K. A. (2009). *Desiring the kingdom: Worship, worldview, and cultural formation.* Grand Rapids: Baker Academic.

Trilling, B. (2010, April). 21st century middle schools: What does success really mean? *Middle Ground, 13*(4), 8–11. http://www.amle.org/Publications/MiddleGround/Articles/April2010/Article2/tabid/2166/Default.aspx

Winerip, M. (2011, April 3). Teenagers speak up for lack of faith. *New York Times.* http://www.nytimes.com/2011/1/04/04/education/04winerip.html?r=1&scp=tenagers%20speak%20up&st=cse

Wolterstorff, N. (2002). *Educating for life: Reflections on Christian teaching and learning.* In G. G. Stronks & C. Joldersma. (Eds.) Grand Rapids: Baker Academic.

CHAPTER 11

IS MEETING
THE DIVERSE NEEDS OF ALL
STUDENTS POSSIBLE?

Gloria Ladson-Billings
University of Wisconsin–Madison

I am sitting in a 2/3 classroom observing a student teacher. I have specifi-cally placed her in this classroom because she has had some struggles and the cooperating teacher is a former student of mine known for her strong teach-ing skills. I notice that the majority of the classroom members are African-American boys. They are energetic and high-spirited. Seated at a table on the far left side of the classroom are three Latina girls who chatter incessantly in Spanish; at another table, all alone sits a rather large (compared to the other children) White boy. He rarely interacts with the other students, keeps his head buried in a book, and shouts out answers (mostly correct) to every ques-tion the teacher poses. A talkative and sassy African-American girl sits near the front of the room and regularly makes it clear that her male counterparts do not intimidate her.

After a few minutes, more students stream in from another class. Two of them have physical handicaps and another tall African-American boy enters loudly and without regard for what the teacher is doing at that moment. One of the students is a twin and he and his twin playfully run in and out of each other's classroom, fooling no one, and annoying the teacher. In one of my post-ob-servation conferences, I learn that the tall White boy is a high functioning

Schooling for Tomorrow's America, pages 149–156

student with Asperger's syndrome. The tall African-American boy has been shot and his mother does not consent to his receiving any type of counseling or therapy.

This classroom is a beehive of activity, lots of it off task and highly unpredictable. One of the few moments of peace and order comes once a week when an African-American man, a local pastor with an imposing presence comes to mentor a group of the boys. His presence provides what the literature calls a "role model" or "father figure" for the boys. His is the only African-American male presence seen regularly at the school and his combination of stern and compassion seem to draw the boys to him.

As I am sitting in the class this particular day I ask myself whether it is reasonable to expect novice teachers to be expert managers and pedagogues in settings like this one. Their experienced teacher is struggling with them. How can we expect newly minted teachers to find success in such classrooms?

THE NATURE OF THE PROBLEM

I relate the aforementioned vignette as a way to help us think about the complexities of teaching in school environments that serve students from a variety of backgrounds and experiences. For many years the notion of "diversity" was a code word for talking simply about race and/or ethnicity. To say one had a diverse class was to say one was not teaching White students. Much of the literature, curriculum materials, and instructional practices were geared toward teaching particular groups of students—African-Americans, Latinos, immigrant students, second language learners, or students with disabilities. But by sitting in the classroom I described, it has become abundantly clear that classrooms are complex organisms. The students bring with them richly textured biographies that go beyond their racial and ethnic categorizations and their teachers bring their own sets of complexities. Somewhere in the nexus of this humanity we are charged with producing literate, numerate, young citizens who are capable of learning more and faster than any generation that has preceded it. This is no small task.

The first challenge to addressing the need to teach all students well is the talent pool from which we are drawing to take on this task. As I sat in the 2/3 classroom, I could not help but reflect on the group of soon to be student teachers I taught each Monday afternoon. They are bright, committed, and quite typical of the U.S. teaching force. They are almost all White, lower-middle to middle income, English monolingual, suburbanites with a strong desire to teach in communities like the ones they grew up in. They may see urban teaching as noble and socially important but it is "too hard" for them. Unfortunately, far too many of them will find themselves taking these "hard" jobs out of economic necessity and their lack of preparedness will show and be a disservice to yet another generation of poor and disenfranchised students, their families, and their communities.

Even in the instances of the growing numbers of alternatively certified teachers who express a strong desire to teach in hard to staff schools we still see poorly prepared teachers who regularly depart from urban schools and classrooms serving poor children of color at an alarmingly high rate. Add to the challenge the fact that current state and federal law regarding public education mandates that all children, regardless of the condition of their schools, the quality of their resources, and the preparation of their teachers, achieve at the same levels of proficiency on standardized tests of reading, writing, and mathematics. The consequences of this high stakes demand were summed up poignantly by a colleague working on value-added assessment of teachers. One of the teachers in his study said something to the effect of, "we are now starting to resent the very children who need us most!" How do we begin to prepare teachers to teach all students in this environment? What solutions can we apply to the problems before us?

Multicultural teacher education has at least a 30-year history (see Banks & Banks, 2003). In 1977, AACTE surveyed 786 member institutions to determine which institutions had courses, a major or minor, or departments in bilingual and/or multicultural education or whether some component of multicultural or bilingual education was included in the foundations or methods courses. Four hundred and forty institutions responded to the survey. And, according to the Commission on Multicultural Education (1978), 48 of the 50 states and the District of Columbia had at least one institution that had either a multicultural component within the foundations or methods course. I include this information to underscore the fact that we have had a tradition of multicultural education in the preparation of teachers for several generations of teachers. Why then, are we having so much difficulty preparing teachers to serve diverse groups of students?

NO EASY ANSWERS

The challenge of teaching *all* students well is not a new one. In the nation's early history, the response was to not attempt to teach them all (see for example Anderson, 1988; Tyack, 1974). Only certain students were deemed worthy of attending school, and these were the only ones we taught. In later years, we used the deep segregation of the society to cordon off Black and Indian children from the White students, and we hardly cared about what was taught in these separate and unequal schools. After the landmark Supreme Court ruling of *Brown versus The Topeka Board of Education*, there were attempts to desegregate the schools and do away with separate facilities. However, over time powerful interests and court rulings found ways to chip away at *Brown* and before we knew it the de facto conditions of segregation were recreated and today Black and Latino school children find themselves more deeply segregated than before. Scholars like Gary Orfield (Orfield & Frankenberg, 2007) argue that if we can break up that deeply entrenched segregation we can improve the achievement level of all students.

In the face of the society's deep resistance to school desegregation or what opponents' call, "social engineering," we have attempted to remedy the problems that students in segregated settings face by recruiting and preparing more teachers of color. And, while that is a worthy goal (indeed, we should have more teachers of color); there is nothing in the scholarly literature to suggest that racial compatibility necessarily means school achievement. If that were the case then most African-American families would rush to enroll their children in Detroit or Washington, DC schools. Many of the alternative certification routes to teaching do an excellent job of recruiting young people of color into the teaching force. But, does their preparation help them survive and thrive in these urban classrooms? The data suggest just the opposite—young teachers of color leave the profession at a higher rate than their White counterparts.

But, let us suppose that we could do a better job of recruiting young people of color into teaching. What will they find when they enroll in their local teacher education programs? The fig leaf covering teacher education is the fact that most teachers educators are old, White, and too far removed from PK–12 teaching to be of much help when it comes to preparing novice teachers for diverse classrooms. Teacher education's "dirty little secret" is that it has not done a very good job of policing itself when it comes to issues of diversity. The sad truth of the academy is that scholars of color are expected to enter it to focus solely on topics of diversity. Thus, teacher education has not created a strong pipeline of diverse scholars who can challenge conventional thinking about what it means to teach diverse groups of students.

In most teacher education programs students encounter a scholar of color teaching the "multicultural" or "diversity" course and sometimes teaching an ESL or bilingual education course. Rarely do they see these scholars as helping them make sense of teaching and learning. Additionally, the very course work that comprises teacher education fails to take up notions of culture and learning in robust and substantive ways. Instead of a "diversity" course, our prospective teachers could benefit from an authentic course on culture (from an anthropological perspective) and how culture impacts learning. Few teacher education programs offer such a course and when they do, they rarely offer them as a program requirement.

So, if the teaching force is not diverse, the teacher educators are not diverse, and the course work does not adequately prepare students to teach a diverse set of students what can we do? Some who advocate for a more market-driven, neo-liberal approach advocate doing away with teacher education altogether (Hess, 2010). These proponents see alternative certification as the most appropriate way to improve teachers and teaching. Indeed, most alternatively certified teachers are placed in school districts serving poor urban and rural students of color, but they too are unprepared to meet the educational needs of these students. Despite excellent Ivy League and other elite college and university degrees these young people struggle with the reality of what it means to teach in classrooms where students and their families have radically different social, economic, and cultural experiences from their own. Former Teach for America alumnae, Sarah Sentilles (2005) describes in graphic detail the limitations of her preparation for the challenge of teaching in Compton, California, one of the state's poorest communities.

In the final section of this essay I present a sliver of hope that helps us address the challenges before us.

Despite her Harvard education Sentilles was not able to overcome the huge issues confronting poor children and their families relegated to the worst school and the mountains of bureaucracy and inefficiency. What Sentilles knew academically had little chance of succeeding in classrooms where students were victims of years of educational neglect. Just putting a "smart" person in the classroom cannot overcome what many urban (and rural) students contend with. In Sentilles own words:

> At Garvey Elementary School, I taught over 30 second graders in a so-called temporary building. Most of these "temporary" buildings have been on campuses in Compton for years. The one I taught in was old. Because the wooden beams across the ceiling were being eaten by termites, a fine layer of wood dust covered the students' desks every morning. Maggots crawled in a cracked and collapsing area of the floor near my desk. One day after school I went to sit in my chair, and it was completely covered in maggots. I was nearly sick. Mice race behind cupboards and bookcases. I trapped six in terrible traps called "glue lounges" given to me by the custodians. The blue metal window coverings on the outsides of the windows were shut permanently, blocking all sunlight. Someone had lost the tool needed to open them, and no one could find another. . . . (p. 72)

The utter lack of regard that we as a nation have for poor children of color cannot be remedied by putting a fresh faced, well-educated young person in the room. We must have a more deliberate and coordinated approach to what has become one of our more pressing social problems.

Some may argue that the Compton situation cited above is an extreme one (and I agree), but suggesting that there are extreme cases does not mean that we do not have widespread problems attempting to educate diverse students. To suggest that there is a problem but that the problem is "not that bad" is a little like suggesting that since slavery was horrible, strict racial segregation was "not that bad." It is bad when African-American and Latino students regularly under-perform in our nation's schools. Most of us know the litany of statistical woes that describe the performance of Black and Brown children in the 25 largest school districts. The racial performance gaps as measured by the National Assessment of Educational Progress (NAEP) for African-American students are between 23 and 26 points. There is a similar difference for Latino students. These students are at a greater risk for school drop out, suspension, and expulsion (Skiba, et al., 2006). But even more telling than the terrible statistics that characterize urban schools (and a growing number of rural schools), is the fact that many African-American and Latino students that attend what we regard as "good" schools have greater achievement disparities than their urban counterparts (see, Minority Student Achievement Network http://msan.wceruw.org/resources/educators.aspx). The Minority Student Achievement Network is a consortium of about 20–25 high performing school districts that have a significant achievement gap between their White students and their Black and/or Brown students. A typical MSAN school district is located in a middle to upper middle-class community, often a college or university town, and prides itself with providing an outstanding public education for its citizens. Because these districts continue to graduate most of their students and to send them directly to high quality post-secondary schools, they are successful in hiding the reality that many African-American and Latino students, regardless of their own middle-class backgrounds, are failing to perform at similarly high levels. Thus, the question of meeting the needs of all students goes beyond the often used sobriquet, "they are coming from a 'culture of poverty.'"

IT'S NOT ALL BAD NEWS

There are a number of objective facts that we know about teacher education that we can do something about. Ingersoll (2003) points out that the number of teachers moving out or changing schools each year almost equals the number of teachers we prepare each year. We also know that teachers assigned to schools serving large numbers of poor children of color are more likely to leave those schools and/or teaching than those assigned to middle income communities serving White children. So, if some schools are hard to staff, we have to make sure that there are incentives for teachers who agree to teach and stay at such schools.

We know that the number of teachers of color entering the field is declining. Indeed, there is an inverse relationship between the race and ethnicity of students in urban classrooms and the teachers who stand before them.

Less than 6% of teachers nation-wide are African-American while many urban school districts have populations of better than 70% students of color. It is here that teacher education must be more aggressive in recruiting and retaining prospective teachers of color. This means that we have to move away from the false dichotomy of equity versus excellence. Instead, we must embrace them as two wonderfully compatible ideas that make our teacher education programs stronger and more competitive.

I do want to point out that I am not assuming any special ethnic or racial skill set linked to teachers of color. There is no empirical evidence that suggests that African-American students achieve at higher levels when they have African-American teachers. Rather, the push for diversifying the teaching force is linked to the benefit *all* students, parents, and teachers will receive by coming into contact with broader perspectives and recognizing the value of diversity to our democracy.

The challenge teacher educators have in developing a more diverse teaching force is doing it when its own ranks are not diverse. Although many teacher education programs advertise themselves as promoting diversity and social justice, the number of teacher educators of color is as dismal as that of the number of teachers of color in K–12 education. With the exception of those employed at the approximately 100 historical Black colleges and universities, few African-Americans are employed as teacher educators. Eighty-eight percent of the full time education professors in the United States are White. Eighty-one percent of those professors are between the ages of 45 and 60 (or older). Only 8% of education professors are faculty of color and of that group about 5% are African-Americans. Until we are willing to take a long hard look at who we bring into teacher education and make change at that level, it may be difficult to recruit and retain prospective teachers of color.

Two weeks before I sat in that 2/3 classroom where both the veteran and novice teacher were struggling to meet all of the students' needs, I sat in a high school in New York. In walked about 22 young men, mostly Black (i.e., African-American, Afro-Caribbean, and African) and Latino. They were well spoken, polite, and disciplined (without being regimented). The group was a cohort of young sophomores who had an opportunity to work together to improve their academic profiles and plan for their post high school futures. Every young man knew his score on the New York State Regents Exam and every one of them was passing. This was a huge turnaround from their freshman year and they were proud of the brotherly bond they had forged with each other. One key to their success was the fact that the principal had successfully recruited a group of Black and Latino male teachers to serve as their core course (i.e., mathematics, science, social studies, and English) teachers and these teachers worked with them regularly to provide additional counseling and tutoring. They challenged each other to do better. At one point during our meeting one student, known as "The Honcho" organized the young men, called them to attention and barked out a command for a "line speak." Immediately, the young men began reciting in unison inspirational poems about taking responsibility for themselves and others, taking charge of their futures, and making good decisions. Their style reminded me of the Black Greek Letter Organizations (i.e., fraternities and sororities) where working together in a spirit of brotherhood is the paramount value.

When I asked what was hard about high school, one young man hesitated, smiled and said, "Actually, nothing about high school is that hard. If you just do your homework and study, you've conquered more than half the battle." His classmates nodded in agreement. "Just doing homework will get you a long way," remarked another boy. What had these youngsters learned that seems so difficult to convey to so many others? How had they learned it? What do we need to do to ensure that more of our students see school as "not that hard?" How can teacher educators help prospective teachers see all students as capable of mastering all that school has to offer? The time I spent with them made me hopeful that success for all of our students is possible—and necessary.

REFERENCES

Anderson, J. (1988). The education of Blacks in the South, 1860–1935. Chapel Hill, NC: University of North Carolina Press.

Banks, J. A., & Banks, C. M. (Eds.). (2003). Handbook of research on multicultural education (2nd ed.). San Francisco: Jossey-Bass.

Commission on Multicultural Education (1978). Directory: Multicultural programs in teacher education institutions in the United States. Washington, DC: American Association of Colleges for Teacher Education.

Hess, F. (2010). The same thing over and over. Cambridge, MA: Harvard University Press.

Ingersoll, R. (2003). Is there really a teacher shortage? Report to the Center for Policy and Research in Education and the Center for the Study of Teaching and Policy. Philadelphia, PA: University of Pennsylvania, Graduate School of Education.

Orfield, G., & Frankenberg, E. (2007). Lessons in integration: Realizing the promise of racial diversity in America's public schools. Charlottesville, VA: University of Virginia Press.

Sentilles, S. (2005). Taught by America: A story of struggle and hope in Compton. Boston: Beacon Press.

Skiba, R., Simmons, A., Ritter, S., Kohler, K., Henderson, M., & Wu, T. (2006). The context of minority disproportionality: Practitioner perspectives on special education referral. Teachers' College Record, 108, 1424–1459.

Tyack, D. (1974). The one best system: A history of American urban education. Cambridge, MA: Harvard University Press.

ABOUT THE CONTRIBUTORS

William Ayers (Bill) became a member of the Laureate Chapter of KDP in 2000. Ayers is a retired Distinguished Professor of Education and Senior University Scholar from the University of Illinois, Chicago Center. He has written extensively about social justice, educational reform, democracy in education and teaching as an intellectual, ethical and political endeavor. His books include: *Teaching Toward Freedom: Moral Commitment and Ethical Action in the Classroom* (2004); *Teaching the Personal and the Political: Essays on Hope and Justice* (1993); *To Teach: The Journey of a Teacher,* which was named the Book of the Year by Kappa Delta Pi in 1993 and the Witten Award for Distinguished Work in Biography and Autobiography in 1995; *A Kind and Just Parent; The Children of Juvenile Court* (1997); and the *Handbook of Social Justice in Education* with Therese Quinn and David Stovall (2008). He has articles published in a wide variety of professional journals. Ayers was founder of the Small Schools Workshop and the Center for Youth and Society in Chicago. He served as Vice President of the American Educational Research Association (AERA) in 2008.

James A. Banks became a member of the Kappa Delta Pi Laureate Chapter in 1997. Banks holds the Kerry and Linda Killinger Endowed Chair in Diversity Studies and is Founding Director of the Center for Multicultural Education at the University of Washington, Seattle. A specialist in social studies and multicultural education, he has published numerous publications in these fields. His most recent book is the eighth edition of *Multicultural Education: Issues and Perspectives,* co-edited with Cherry A. McGee

Schooling for Tomorrow's America, pages 157–163
Copyright © 2014 by Information Age Publishing

Banks. His other publications include *Teaching Strategies for Ethnic Studies*, eighth ed. (2008) and *Cultural Diversity and Education: Foundations, Curriculum and Teaching*, fifth ed. (2005). He is editor of the *Routledge International Companion to Multicultural Education* and the *Encyclopedia of Diversity in Education* (4 volumes), published by Sage in 2012. Professor Banks' work in multicultural education is known and influential throughout the world. His books have been translated into Greek, Japanese, Chinese, and Korean. He was a Spencer Fellow at the Center for Advanced Study in the Behavioral Sciences at Stanford in 2005–2006, and the Tisch Distinguished Visiting Professor at Teachers College, Columbia University in 2007. Banks is a member of the National Academy of Education, a Fellow of the American Educational Research Association (AERA), and a past President of AERA and of the National Council for the Social Studies (NCSS).

David Berliner became a member of the Kappa Delta Pi Laureate Chapter in 1997. Berliner is the Regent's Professor Emeritus of the Mary Lou Fulton Teachers College at Arizona State University, Tempe. His areas of research and publications focused on educational psychology and the behavioral sciences. A prolific writer, his writing included: *The Manufactured Crisis: Myths, Fraud, and the Attack on America's Public Schools* (with B. J. Biddle, 1996); *Putting Research to Work in Your Schools* (with Ursula Casanova, 1996); *Collateral Damage: How High Stakes Testing Corrupts America's Schools* (with Sharon Nichols, 2007); and he edited (with Robert Calfee) the first *Handbook of Educational Psychology* (1996). He is the author of over 200 book chapters and articles in various professional journals. Berliner also served as president of both the American Educational Research Association (AERA) and the Division of Educational Psychology of the American Psychological Association. He is also the recipient of numerous awards for his contributions to APA, AERA, and NEA (National Education Association).

Marilyn Cochran-Smith became a member of the Kappa Delta Pi Laureate Chapter in 2003. Cochran-Smith is the Cawthorne Professor of Teacher Education and Director of the Doctoral Program in Curriculum and Instruction at the Lynch School of Education, Boston College. Cochran-Smith is a frequent presenter nationally and internationally and is widely known for her work in teacher education, research, practice and policy. She has published nine books, five of which have won national awards, including: *Inquiry as Stance: Practitioner Research in the Next Generation* (with Susan Lytle, 2009); *Walking the Road: Race, Diversity and Social Justice in Education* (2004); *Policy, Practice and Politics in Teacher Education: Editorial from the Journal of Teacher Education* (2006); *The Making of a Reader* (1984); and *Learning to Write Differently: Beginning Writers and Word Processing* (with Cynthia Paris and Jessica Kahn, 1991). She has also published over 175 articles, chapters

and editorials in the professional literature on social justice, practitioner research, and teacher education research, practice and policy. From 2000 to
2006, she was the chief editor of the *Journal of Teacher Education*. Currently,
she is a co-editor with Susan Lytle of the Teachers College Press book series
on Practitioner Inquiry. She is an elected member of the National Academy
of Education and a Fellow of the American Educational Research Association (AERA). She was President of AERA in 2004–2005.

Barbara Day became a member of the Laureate Chapter of Kappa Delta Pi
in 2006. Day is currently Professor and Chair, Curriculum and Instruction in
the School of Education at the University of North Carolina at Chapel Hill. A
former teacher, principal, and assistant superintendent of schools, she served
as the Chair of Early Childhood Education, Elementary Education, Teaching
and Learning at the University of North Carolina at Chapel Hill. Day has
studied education in many parts of the world: Great Britain, the Scandinavian
countries, Germany, Switzerland, Russia, China, Korea, Singapore, Japan,
and Africa. Her textbooks and publications include, *Open Learning in Early
Childhood Education* (1975), *Good Schools for Young Children, 5th ed.* (1978 with
Leeper and Witherspoon), *Early Childhood Education: Curriculum Organization
and Classroom Management* (1983 with Drake), *Early Childhood Education: Creative Learning, 3rd ed.* (1988), and *Teaching and Learning in the New Millennium*
(1999). Day has served as President of The Association for Supervision and
Curriculum Development, Kappa Delta Pi, and Delta Kappa Gamma Society International. Extremely active in Delta Kappa Gamma, she spearheaded
a drive in North Carolina for a new Women's Executive Leadership Training Program, served as Chair of the International Research Committee and
served as editor of the book, *Education for the 21st century. Key Issues: Leadership, Literacy, Legislation, and Learning*. Currently, she serves as a member of
Delta Kappa Gamma's Expansion Committee. Day is also very involved in service to the Episcopal Church and completed her Doctoral Ministry Degree at
Virginia Theological Seminary in Alexandria, Virginia.

O. L. Davis, Jr., became a member of the Laureate Chapter of Kappa Delta
Pi in 1994. He is the Catherine Mae Parker Centennial Professor of Curriculum and Instruction Emeritus in the College of Education, The University of Texas at Austin. He received his PhD in Curriculum and Teaching
from the George Peabody College for Teachers (1958), and has held teaching and administrative posts in Texas and Tennessee schools. His areas of
specialization include curriculum practice and theory, social studies education practice and theory, and curriculum history. A prolific author, he has
published more than 160 research reports and interpretive analyses in a
variety of scholarly journals, is the senior author of a series of elementary
school social studies textbooks, and has been editor or co-editor of more

than 25 books. He has served as a member of the editorial boards of *The Educational Forum, The Curriculum Journal,* and *Theory and Research in Social Education.* He has served as Associate Editor for, the *American Educational Research Journal;* and as Editor for, *Journal of Curriculum and Supervision.* He has been: President, ASCD (1980–81); Vice-President, Division B (Curriculum Studies) AERA (1973–1974); President, Kappa Delta Pi, (1978–1980) and Counselor of Delta Chapter of KDP for 40 years (1967–2007); founding member and President, Society for the Study of Curriculum History (1978–1980) and founding President, AATC (1993–94). He received Distinguished Alumnus Awards from the University of North Texas and Peabody College, Vanderbilt University, and the Distinguished Faculty Award, College of Education, The University of Texas at Austin. In 1996, AERA presented him with a Citation for Distinguished Contributions to Curriculum Studies and the National Council for the Social Studies presented him with its first Exemplary Award for Distinguished Research in Social Studies Education and, it's Career Research Award in Social Studies Education. In 2003, The Society of Professors of Education presented him with the Mary Anne Raywid Award for his distinguished scholarship in education.

Elizabeth De Gaynor is a doctoral student at Duke Divinity School, with a focus on Theology and Pedagogy. She is currently doing ethnographic research at schools in Michigan. Her publications include a chapter, "The Word: Creative and Poetic" in *Holy Things for Youth Ministry: Thirteen Practical Sessions,* Brian Hardesty-Crouch, Editor (Cleveland: Pilgrim Press, 2011), and an article with Dr. Barbara Day in the *Delta Kappa Gamma Bulletin* (January 2011), "Annotated Bibliography of Materials for Spirituality in the Classroom: Fostering Social and Emotional Leaning and Developing Moral Schools." She has presented at numerous conferences, including a paper at the Education as Formation conference, sponsored by the Kuyers Institute for Christian Teaching and Learning: "There is No Such Thing as a Neutral Educational Process" (October 2011), and a workshop with Dr. Barbara Day at North Carolina Eta State Organization Conference, sponsored by Delta Kappa Gamma Society International: "Religion and Spirituality in the Public High School Classroom (April 2010). She is a former department chair and high school English teacher at The Covenant School (Charlottesville, VA).

Marcella L. Kysilka is Professor Emerita of the College of Education at the University of Central Florida. Marcella became a member of Delta Chapter of Kappa Delta Pi in 1968, while completing her doctoral degree in Curriculum and Instruction at the University of Texas at Austin. Upon graduation, she became a charter faculty member in the College of Education at the University of Central Florida. She remained at UCF for 37 years serving in a variety of positions: Professor, Assistant Dean of Academic Affairs, Director of the Institute for Research and Program Development in the College of Education, and Director of the Doctoral Program in Curriculum and Instruction. Very active in her professional associations at state, national and international levels, she served in a variety of Leadership roles in AERA, ASCD, ISATT, and AATC where she was Executive Director from 1991-2003. Her activities in Kappa Delta Pi were numerous: Budget Committee Member and chair, Vice President for Chapter Development, President-Elect, President, Past-President, Chair, Convocation Committee, Academic Editor, *Educational Forum*, Educational Foundation Board and Chair 2006-2011. She published numerous articles and books and received awards for her scholarship and service including Outstanding Professor and/or Researcher (seven times) from UCF. In 2011 she received the first Dr. Truman L. Kelley Award for Scholarship Excellence from Kappa Delta Pi.

Gloria Ladson-Billings became a member of the Kappa Delta Pi Laureate Chapter in 2009. Ladson-Billings holds the Kellner Family Chair in Urban Education and is Professor of Curriculum and Instruction and Educational Policy Studies at the University of Wisconsin–Madison. Her areas of specialty are cultural studies, critical race theory applied to education and educational anthropology. A prolific writer, she has published numerous articles in a variety of professional journals as well as entries in both the *Handbook of Research on Multicultural Education, 2nd Ed.* and *The Sage Handbook of Qualitative Research, 3rd Ed.* Additional books include: *The Dreamkeeper: Successful Teachers of African American Children* (2009); *Foundations of Critical Race Theory in Education* (2009 with E. Taylor & d. Gillborn); Educational Research in the *Public Interest: Social Justice, Action and Policy* (2006, with W. Tate), and *Crossing Over to Canaan: The Journey of New Teachers in Diverse Classrooms* (2001). Her most recent book is *Beyond the Big House: African American Educators on Teacher Education (2005)*. Ladson-Billings received an Honorary Doctorate from Umeå University, Sweden, the George and Louise Spindler Award from the Council on Anthropology and Education (2004), the Palmer O. Johnson Award for Educational Research (1995) from the American Education Research Association (AERA) and served as President of AERA in 2005–2006.

Ann Lieberman became a member of the Kappa Delta Pi Laureate chapter in 1995. Currently, she is Professor Emerita of Education at Teachers College, Columbia University, in New York. She previously was a Senior Scholar at the Carnegie Foundation for the Advancement of Teaching. Lieberman's research has been in the areas of teacher development and leadership, collaborative research, school-university partnerships, and understanding educational change. She is the author or co-author of a number of professional books. Her most recent book, written with Linda Darling-Hammond is, *Teacher Education around the World: Changing Policies and Practices* (2012). Other books include, *Mentoring Teacher: Navigating the Real world Tensions* (with Susan Hanson, Janet Glass and Ellen Moire (2011); *How Teachers Become Leaders* with Linda Friedrich (2010); Editor, *The Roots of Education Change; International Handbook of Educational Change* (2005). *Teacher Leadership* with Lynne Miller (2004), and *Inside the National Writing Project: Connecting Network Learning and Classroom Teaching* with Diane Wood (2003). In additional she has published numerous articles in professional journals. Lieberman has served on many national and international advisory boards including the United Federation of Teachers and the National Education Association. She is past president of the American Educational Research Association and has been recognized with an Honorary Degree from California State University at Northridge.

Deborah Meier became a Kappa Delta Pi Laureate in 2000. Meier is a Senior Scholar at Steinhardt School of Education, New York University and Board member and Director of the New Ventures at Mission Hill School in Boston. She is also Director and Advisor to Forum of Democracy and Education, serves on the Board of the Coalition of Essential Schools, is a founding member of the National Board of Professional Teaching Standards, the founder and teacher-director of a network of highly successful public elementary schools in East Harlem, and of Central Park East Secondary school, a high school where 90% of the entering students go on to college. These schools served predominantly low-income African-American and Latino students in New York. Her writings include: *The Power of Their Ideas, Lessons to America from a Small School in Harlem* (1995); *Will Standards Save Public Education?* (2000); *In Schools We Trust* (2002); *Keeping Schools with Ted and Nancy Sizer* (2004); and *Many Children Left Behind* (2004). Her latest book is *Playing for Keeps: Life and Learning on a Public School Playground* (2010) with Brenda Engel and Beth Taylor. Deborah Meier has been a recipient of a MacArthur Fellowship and several honorary degrees.

Nel Noddings became a Kappa Delta Pi Laureate in 1994. She is currently the Lee L. Jacks Professor Emerita of Child Education at Stanford University in Palo Alto, California. Her writings have been highly influential in the areas of ethics of care and their relationship to schooling, welfare, and to teaching and learning. She is a former elementary teacher, a high school mathematics teacher and public school administrator. At Stanford, she was recognized as an outstanding teacher and served as acting Dean of the College of Education. On retiring from Stanford in 1998, she taught at Columbia University, Colgate University, and the University of Southern Maine. She has received numerous awards and recognitions from professional organizations and universities. Her publications include: *Caring: A Feminine Approach to Ethics and Moral Education* (1984); *Women and Evil* (1989); *The Challenge to Care in School* (1992) *Educating Moral People* (2002); *Happiness in Education* (2003); along with numerous articles in a variety of profession journals. She is former president of the Philosophy of Education Society and the John Dewey Society.

Christine Power is a doctoral student at the Lynch School of Education at Boston College. Her research interests include teacher education policy and teaching for social justice. Prior to coming to Boston College, Power taught world and United States history in Boston-area schools for over ten years. In addition to numerous regional and national conferences presentations on the topics of equity in education and teacher education policy, Power works frequently with elementary and secondary teachers in curriculum and instructional development. Her recent publications include co-authored articles in Education Leadership, Journal of Education, Educational Forum and Teachers College Record.

Alan H. Schoenfeld became a member of the Laureate Chapter of KDP in 2006. Currently the Elizabeth and Edward Conner Chair in Education at the University of California, Berkeley Graduate School and Professor of Cognition and Development, his areas of specialization include: Mathematics Education; Assessment and Educational Measurement; Cognitive Development; Educational Equity; Research Methods; and School Culture. Schoenfeld's research deals with thinking, teaching, and learning. Schoenfeld led the Balanced Assessment project and was one of the leaders of the NSF sponsored center for Diversity in Mathematics Education. He was lead author for grades 9–12 of the National Council of Teachers of Mathematics; *Principles and Standards for School Mathematics*. He was one of the founding editors of *Research in Collegiate Mathematics Education,* and has served as associate editor of *Cognition and Instruction*. He has served as senior advisor to the Educational Human Resources Directorate of the National Science Foundation and senior content advisor to the What Works Clearinghouse. His recent book (2010), *How We Think: A Theory of Goal-oriented Decision Making and its Educational Applications* describes the theory and establishes a framework for thinking about issues of teachers' professional growth and development. He is a prolific author of professional articles and books. He received the Senior Scholar Award, Special Interest Group for Research in Mathematics Education of AREA and the Lester R. Ford Award, Mathematical Association of American. He was President of AERA (1998), is a Fellow of the AAAS (2001), and served as distinguished lecturer: The American Society for Engineering Education, The University of Michigan; North Carolina State University; The University of Washington; and George Washington University and currently serves as Special Professor, University of Nottingham.

CPSIA information can be obtained at www.ICGtesting.com
Printed in the USA
LVOW10s1958040414

380431LV00003B/17/P